# The
# LAST
# GOOD
# LIGHT

*A Southern Memoir*

LINDA CARROLL BARNES

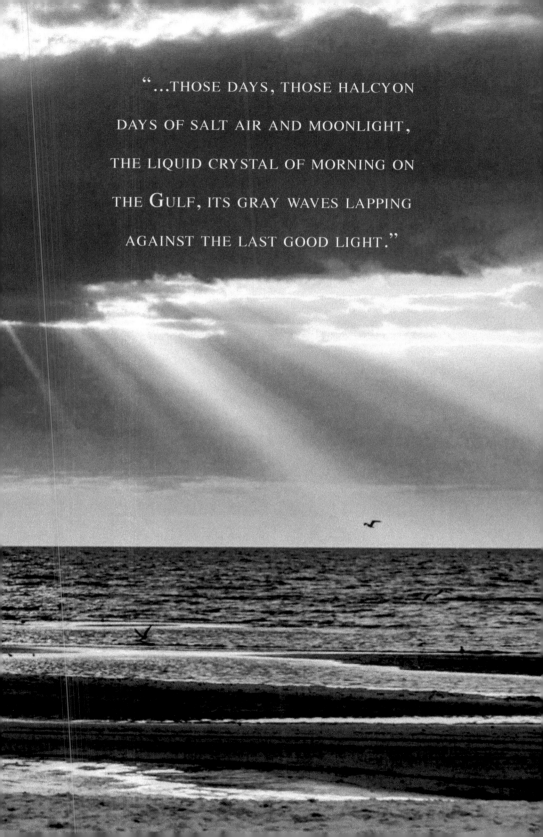

"...THOSE DAYS, THOSE HALCYON DAYS OF SALT AIR AND MOONLIGHT, THE LIQUID CRYSTAL OF MORNING ON THE GULF, ITS GRAY WAVES LAPPING AGAINST THE LAST GOOD LIGHT."

Cover photo, historic "Oldfields" in Gautier, MS, and photo pages 156-157: Used by permission of John Majure

Photo of the Friendship House, page 57: Used by permission of John Cuevas

Photo of the Weejuns, page 70: Used by permission of the Benefield family and band members (left to right in the picture) Woo Sheely, Charlie Wood, Ricky Fant, (the late) George White and Dennis Braun

Coast photos, pages 30, 50, 78, 110, 122, 124, and 136: Used by permission of the Ron Maxie family

Coast photos, Title pages, 48, 54, 62, 64, 90, and 94: Used by permission of Jason Taylor

Photos pages 72 and 133: Used by permission of Joan McCool

Author's portrait, page 152: Used by permission of Jason Ulsrud

Photos pages 74 and 77: Used by permission of Pete Snell

Photos pages 22, 45, 61, 88, 112, 113, 134, 140 and 149: Property of the author

Photos pages x, 4, 12, 16, 18, 39, 80, 96, 101, 116, and 121: iStockphoto.com

Photo page 32: "Beautiful America" stock photo

Photo 5961130, page 109, © Thomas Cannon l Dreamstime.com

Photo pages 85, 130, 135 provided by Clyde Adams

Cover and interior design: Clyde Adams, www.clydeadamsbooks.com

ISBN: Hardback - 979-8-9871955-1-2   Softback - 979-8-9871955-0-5

MY FRIENDS

FROM THE

MISSISSIPPI GULF COAST,

THIS IS FOR YOU.

# CONTENTS

# FOREWORD

When we are born, we have no control over where we are born or to whom we are born. Most of us know home from our beginnings.

This is the true story of a young girl born into an unsettled family who at a young age was shuttled west to California, then moved to the Big Easy living in the French Quarter before she finally found home on her next move.

Like the ever-wandering gypsy, she found the place she would call home to be a magical place steeped in pre-colonial America's past on the shimmering waters of the Gulf of Mexico.

It was a magnificent place, more beautiful than anything she had ever seen, with giant oak trees, Spanish moss and sweet magnolias that grew to the water's edge. This land was first occupied by ancient Native Americans. A land that witnessed the first French explorers claim the place that would lead to the settlements of Mobile and New Orleans. It was an area infused with cultural influences from France, Spain and Eastern European countries. It was among our country's first melting pots.

This is her story, and how she was forever changed. It was a journey that would change her attitude about life and its purpose. Finally, she was home in more ways than one. As John Milton wrote of Paradise Lost, she writes of Paradise found. Now she counts herself as among the luckiest people on earth.

Ronnie Bell
*former newspaper publisher, award winning columnist*
*and creator of the Lake Magazine*

# INTRODUCTION

I remember the first morning, the very first time I saw it. The road sign read, "Welcome to Mississippi." It stood out like a bright billboard advertising an exciting new attraction. The road we were traveling went straight into Mississippi, leaving Louisiana and the Pearl River vanishing slowly behind us. As far as I could see, narrow determined channels struggled to break free from a tangled marsh, drifting through expansive grasses where the newly liberated waters became a world of silent pools dotted by a continuous chain of green islands.

I felt the first effects of this place in the benign, absorbing way of unknown places, imperceptibly mingling with the old smell of fish camps and damp cypress knees rising like gnarled old men from dark primal waters. An earthiness in the air announced Mississippi, the scent of home, like a fence of honeysuckle in the warm soil of late afternoon. Sultry and penetrating, it hung low over miles of serpentine rivers and bayous, their watery shadows escaping a decomposing wilderness, twisting and turning on their way to the Gulf.

Gradually, the pervasive smells faded reluctantly away, and the last decadent hints of earth and water were aggressively replaced by other scents that lived here. The intensity of jasmine, magnolias and sweet olive drifted in a fragrant evolution over lush green boundaries, liberally decanted in the first whispers of salt winds carrying with them the smell of the sea.

I drifted slowly among them like an apparition looking for a home, following a road that emerged at last into southern greenery and rolling, blue-gray waves. I came to earth gradually, descending into a paradise of palm trees and moss covered oaks on a white ribbon of glittering sand, a dream world at the edge of the Gulf. There were other residents already here occupying this ground, small constellations of amiable people wholly complicit in sustaining the comfortable balance of a transcendent atmosphere.

The Mississippi Coast was a ghost-like illusion defined by emerging images that I saw unfolding in front of me like a movie, minute by minute. Part of me believed this was a real place. It felt like it was a real place. But the biggest part of me clung to the illusion because it was easier and safer. There was a price to pay if I let this world become too real. Ambient scenery moved inexorably across the wide screen of my little illusion, my imaginary movie that hypnotically drew me further and further into an undisguised typecasting. I began to feel that I fit perfectly into the script, and that my character and this setting were a definite part of this convenient arrangement.

Warm nights and tentative days encouraged me to flow along with them, floating in and out of a pliable background while I waited to feel like I belonged here. The feeling of belonging always took time, and I was surprised one day when I noticed it waiting for me among the long shrouded curves of oak trees dripping moss in the morning mist rising on a gray Gulf. I saw it again later in a fiery sunset melting over the hard edge of a blue horizon. Mississippi was actually real, and I actually belonged here on this white beach, breathing warm salt air under a brilliant sky. It was alright to believe it now.

Before I came here, in other places far away, I had a few brief glimpses of what it might feel like to actually belong somewhere. I saw signs of it in most of the people I knew who seemed so easily at home all of the time, something I could only dream of. Mostly, it was just something I naively wished for, like a fairytale. Belonging seemed like one of those illusive personal benefits that would probably remain the exclusive property of other people unless my circumstances were altered significantly. Then one day, surprisingly and without any warning, that is exactly what happened. My perpetually dormant young life erupted in a smoldering avalanche of change, and suddenly, in the supernatural way that happens only in fairy tales, I stepped into the world of my dreams.

## Chapter 1

# A BEGINNING

I didn't know when my eyes opened on that chilly Oklahoma morning, looking out at the first yellow jonquils among the fallen leaves, or when I ate my white bread toast, or when we rode downtown to the station, that liberation was coming. It came as it often does, in the form of a person. In this case, it meant a person with a point of view that was unerringly generous and

pleasantly elastic, qualities that brought with them an immediate and appealing warmth. It arrived dressed in gray traveling clothes, in a busy train station filled with harried travelers dodging among heavy luggage carts. The uniformed porters moved methodically up and down the platform, checking their watches and struggling against the throng of the arriving and the departing.

The heat rising from the engine became a cloud-like mist faintly obscuring the faces of the descending passengers. The surreal moment hung in the air for an instant, just long enough for me to wonder if our visitor had actually come. Finally, a gray figure and her traveling case appeared, pausing in the doorway. She emerged like a translucent ghost, stepping down from the train, looking up and down the platform for familiar faces, our faces, and then walked smiling toward us. Someone had come to see us, and we were here to welcome her and take her home with us. My aunt was my grandmother's sister, an ample, jolly woman who smiled easily and was not tedious to be around. These were qualities with which I was somewhat unfamiliar. I had only casually noticed them in the lives of others, and I was continually curious about their absence in our own immediate family. My aunt seemed to actually like me, and because of her soft, unpretentious manner I found her very appealing. We gathered her and her luggage into our gray Buick and wound our way from the train station into the flow of morning traffic. The visit began in the customary way, and there were no signs that it might be uncustomary at all.

I remember the vivid intensity of my childhood thoughts. I seemed to be searching for something even then. When I was eleven or twelve years old, I had the sense that I was looking for my people, and so far had not found them. I never managed to feel quite at home anywhere, more like a visitor or inmate wandering in a strange landscape among ornamental foliage. Lying for hours in the warm grass of Oklahoma summer, my mind was free to drift in the lazy, harmless way of children. Looking up at the swollen white clouds moving higher and higher across sky, I was just waiting to see if I might feel the first faint, illusive sense of belonging.

I wondered about God, whether He was real, and I thought about the kindhearted ladies at church with their flannel boards telling the stories of Abraham, Moses, David, Elijah and all the other Bible characters. These figures had a place where they belonged. They lived securely in their felt lined box and moved about on the large, flannel surface when it was time to tell their stories. It was entirely predictable, and it never changed. I found this very comforting, as if my own identity might lie safely in that same box with the felt figures. We all lived there together joined by a pleasant sameness.

Expectations are dangerous things. It was clear to me pretty early that disappointment was the direct result of rash expectations, often ending in bitter tears and unsympathetic exchanges which turned out badly. I became determined to not expect very much. It was just much safer and saved me a lot of trouble. I did manage to still be a little hopeful on the inside however, which was rewarded eventually by an event entirely unexpected. It marked both an end and a beginning. My father went away. This happened a few times when he found work in other cities, and then later when there were separations between my parents. This time, his leaving would be different. I always felt the effects of his absence deeply, as if the wind of change left a chill in our house, an empty place where warmth had been. The kindest thing to say about our fragmented family life was that my parents were two people on conflicting journeys resulting in a significant and entirely predictable cold war. It was the usual kind, where a few casualties are expected. We had all been casualties for as long as I could remember, but apparently we had gotten used to it.

The various separations continued throughout all my years at home, and we did our best to adjust to them. When these new circumstances arrived it meant that, fundamentally, life for me would now change. On a gray, uninteresting day still wrapped in the chill of winter, a door opened into what would be my new future. Sometime during the week of my aunt's visit, unknown and unimagined by me, a plan was made and consented to. I would go and live with her in California, and we would leave on Friday. The importance of the moment was lost on me, and it was impossible for me to know that the coming days would entirely change my life.

I was thirteen then, the age of long gangly legs and painful insecurities. So far, life had been a series of different destinations in Arkansas, Oklahoma, Louisiana, Texas and California, a transient existence which lent itself to my acquired tendency toward low expectations. I felt that I had only been given a small speaking part in my own life. There was little hope of a grander leading role later on, and acclaim of any sort felt very much out of reach. I knew my aunt fairly well and saw her when she came on her yearly visits. I was a little unsure why I was the object of her attention, but she noticed me and always sat me down at our green formica kitchen table, chatting with me in her mild and disarming way.

For some reason it didn't seem strange to go away with her. It was more like the prospect of an extended holiday, and I was quite used to saying goodbye. It was something I had done many times. Days before, my father had already said goodbye to me, but as the train pulled slowly away I imagined him standing there, and my last small wave to him. I knew well that look on his face, a little worn but still a half smile, as if I was just going off for a movie and ice cream. He always called me "baby," and I already missed hearing his voice saying it. Mine was a familiar sadness, tired now from years of repetition, and every time he went away a little more of the light went out of my life. It would be some time before I saw him again.

My trip to California with my aunt did not seem quite real until we climbed up the heavy metal steps and got on the train. I started being hopeful a few days before when I packed my clothes, and I was even more excited when the porters began loading our luggage. The first sounds of the engine as the cars clanked together were the best, leaving me unsteady when the slow forward motion began. It meant I had been invited somewhere, and I was really going. That sudden sensation of movement gave me a small feeling of exhilaration I have never experienced anywhere else. When I see a train highballing along the tracks or smell that combination of oil and hot steel, it affects me, even now. The train installed itself into my senses and into my life with a feeling that has never left me.

The sound of the rocking cars as we rolled along the track was incredibly soothing. There was no danger of anything being other than exactly what it should be. This brought with it a delicious sense of freedom entirely unknown to me. I started very quickly to feel at home on that train. On the long days of our trip I made friends with some of the passengers, conductors and waiters in the dining car. It was the dining car that in many ways, changed my life.

My father had at least one passion in life that I knew of, and he excelled at it. Because he loved and played golf, I was fortunate, very fortunate, to have a rich association with the advantages of life at the country club. I loved the atmosphere, the calm ease inside the pro shop and the displays of bright golf sweaters and hats. Impressive clubs and colorful bags filled an entire wall beside dark, paneled doors opening into a ballroom used for banquets and club dances. A long bank of windows surrounded the main lounge with a view of the pool and the 18th green. Players sat here in deep maroon leather club chairs talking about their game, or they had drinks downstairs in the 19th Hole. The environment of the club suited me perfectly because I had a great appreciation for order. But most of all, I had an appreciation for the unfailingly cordial conversation that lived here along with it.

*"...as the train pulled slowly away I imagined him standing there, and my last small wave to him."*

I looked everywhere for symmetry. The country club was an object of such perfection, with starched white cloths and silver laid with precision in the dining rooms. The staff, attentive to the needs and expectations of everyone, created splendid works of art on the week-end buffet tables. Rare roast beef and sliced ham, long platters of asparagus and green beans, voluminous au gratin potatoes, at least ten different salads, six kinds of pie and warmers full of soft, pillowy rolls covered tables filling the entire end of the dining room. I had never seen tuna fish salad shaped into the form of a large fish with olive slices for eyes and thin slivers of cucumber for scales.

It impressed me. Very possibly, the joy of food in its infant stage began for me here. It was very different from the tv dinners, cereal and pop-tarts in our kitchen at home.

For lunch at the clubhouse I was always allowed to have a club sandwich accompanied by the drink favored by all of us, something called a "Roy Rogers," a sort of virginal Tom Collins. It was essentially ginger ale served in a tall high ball glass with the perfect amount of machine made ice, garnished with two cherries and a long straw. It seemed very grown-up and always arrived perfectly served on a tray with small white cocktail napkins emblazoned with the club logo.

I got to wear pretty dresses to club dances, play gin-rummy with my friends during the day and Bingo on Saturday nights. A large ice sculpture of a swan or something like it was always brought out to the 18th green by the clubhouse for us to gather around and celebrate the winners of a week-end tournament. It was a ritual of happy people doing something they all loved, and it was very easy to feel at home surrounded by so much beauty and pleasantness.

I could see right away the world of the dining car was characterized by exactly these same things. It was a sort of country club on wheels only with more starch and better silver, which was why the first second I stepped into it, I felt so completely at home. I felt more at home there than I ever felt in my own living room. It didn't occur to me to question why the alternate world of the country club and the portable world of the dining car could be so appealing and so welcoming. They just were. I could see right away some superior signs in the impeccably white uniforms of the waiters, the heavier silver and the small bouquet of flowers on each table.

Anyone who has dined on a moving train can appreciate how difficult it is to serve coffee, tea and steaming plates of food, but these men with their ready smiles did it everyday. They made the difficult seem easy and became my "almost friends," securing for my aunt and me the best table with the best views, extra crackers, extra butter, extra rolls, extra everything, and I was very sad at the end to leave them.

The joy of the dining car was my first discovery, and tea with the barest sliver of lemon that my aunt poured from a small gleaming silver pot into heavy white cups. I was its captive now, and I would drink tea almost like a dying man somewhere, anywhere, and I would always think of her. I was fascinated by the amber, translucent tea itself, the cup framed against the stark white cloth with a shining silver spoon set against it. My first cup of tea in the dining car became a happy pastime for my aunt and me about mid-morning each day, the train rocking gently along the sloping hills, forests, prairies or wherever we happened to be. We made our way to our destination through the long train of passenger cars joined by the somewhat complicated attachment that held them tightly against each other. The cars were filled with people going west as we were and heading to places like Phoenix or Los Angeles. The dining car was usually almost empty by now. We had our morning tea quietly talking just to each other, and being with my aunt made me feel increasingly secure.

In addition to my introduction to tea, my aunt reinvented breakfast for me. There would never again be pop-tarts and cold cereal. She guided me to poached eggs and English muffins with orange marmalade. For the first time, I met pink grapefruit, cut in half, sprinkled with sugar and garnished with a cherry in the center.

For some reason, I was really attracted to that grapefruit, and I was amazed to find that in California they were everywhere, even hanging in the trees.

The atmosphere of the train was wonderfully reliable, and it was far away from the chill winds behind me and the unfortunate, dark, recurring moods of my mother. Her moods had a grim and predictable sameness. They would simply turn without any warning, without any possibility of defense, and take away, absolutely, any small remnants of happiness surviving there. Over time I had gotten used to the unavoidable currents of subtraction. I did wonder sometimes how much of me had already been subtracted, and how much might actually be left. But riding along in the slowly rocking cars, the dark undercurrents that had seemed so tenacious began to fade from my consciousness until they seemed a million miles away.

When I sat beside my aunt on our reclining seats or in the glass dome car looking out the windows of the swaying train, whole new worlds flashed by. I looked at them and everything around me with inquisitive, hopeful eyes like those of a pioneer. We traveled through a seamless countryside populated by families with enthusiastic children who waved at the train from a green station wagon or a battered old Packard with fishing poles sticking out of the windows. Bags of feed and bales of hay filled the back of an old black Ford pick-up parked by a feed store, the men in over-alls leaned against it, talking.

It was a pleasant thing, this passing view of other peoples lives. Cars of every description waited patiently for our train to pass, and I wondered about the people inside that I would never know. Were they going off to have a picnic with a basket of fried chicken? Did they live in a yellow house behind a picket fence with a gray cat asleep by the front door? When darkness came, would they sit laughing together at a kitchen table? I had the oddest need to assign these unidentifiable faces a place in my memory, as if I might someday want to visit them again.

As we went on, there were signs of the frontier West, evidence in the purple distance of ranches with cattle and horses and cowboys. I felt the midnight chill of the tumbledown stop-over stations, the passengers laden with bags as they disappeared into the cold darkness of a New Mexico night, the platform becoming empty and lifeless after they had gone. Other dwellings fought to survive here. Outlined sometimes against the horizon, battered homesteads, ruins now, sagged half covered by struggling old roses planted by someone long ago. The decaying shelters were alive once with people and families. They came out here for a new life. Where had they gone? Did they die out here? Did their dream of settling the West die with them? Before the railroad came, an eternity of inaccessible land reached wide here in every direction, and I thought the ground must be full of stories.

I wanted to travel on and on, and I would have, gladly. I never tired of the constantly changing display of crowded rail yards, rustic wilderness or charming, small towns. We had come to the end of the line though. Farther west, the way would be barred by the blue waves of the Pacific. I wasn't ready for the trip to be over, not nearly ready. In the early morning

*"I looked out the window, thinking it might be the last time I ever felt this way."*

semi-darkness of Barstow, when I was still half asleep and trying to remember exactly where I was, we had a long stop. Arriving passengers burdened with luggage finally boarded, and our train pulled away from the station in its slow, unhurried way. Steadily rocking along the tracks, it wound through a changing panorama of trees and greenery that were here to welcome it. The train had come home and brought us with it.

I was so used to daily life on the train that it seemed like a long portable home on wheels, a comfortable world full of predictable experiences and familiar people that I had grown to care for. Now this pleasantness was slowly coming to an end. I would miss it all: the soothing sound of the track, a pale dawn rising behind a red desert plateau, the satisfying smells of early morning in the dining car and friendly conversation with the others in this transitory world.

Dependable to the last, the train seemed to know it was reaching the final stretch, carrying me safely into my invisible future and preparing to deposit me faithfully at the station. I looked out the window, thinking it might be the last time I ever felt this way, the last time I looked out at my new surroundings merely as an observer. The world outside demanded so much more once a person stepped down into it.

The train moved slowly, gradually coming to its final stop while my aunt and I gathered our things. We crowded through the doorway together with the other passengers, spilling onto the platform in the warm, grove-scented air of southern California. Leaving our movable home behind us, we all converged in the long passageway to collect our luggage and then slowly began disappearing from the station into a bright blue morning.

I took one last look back at the friendly cars and left a small piece of myself behind, staying on board as a grateful and permanent passenger. The daily exhilaration of travel, grand scenery, tea and marmalade and starched white tablecloths never really left me. The train had been my temporary home for all those long miles and I was attached to it now. I could never possibly be separated from its influence.

## Chapter 2

# THE GROVES

1961 was an innocent year in southern California, when things were a shimmering perfection, and this refuge of permanent warmth and lush beauty was one long, sunshine-filled dream. It was a dream that I lived in and against which I now measured all other places. My aunt and I arrived on the train, and finally, after all of those pleasant mornings in the dining car and endless views of sun drenched scenery, we were home. The train that brought us all the long miles from Oklahoma slowly pulled away from the station and left us standing in a shady world of towering oaks and orange groves. My uncle came to meet us at the train station and took us the last miles to their house, my new home. I realized as we passed through the miles of orange groves, that I had arrived in heaven or something very nearly like it.

The house was one of several ranch style homes that hugged the edge of two worlds, the leafy streets of town, and the groves that stretched on forever. It was a slice of paradise, and I now had a place in it. Like others in the small neighborhood, the house was almost new. Not large or pretentious, it sat comfortably on a small lawn bordered by tall colorful cannas and my favorite, the ice plant.

My aunt always packed with great economy, and I had only two standard bags and a train case, so unloading our luggage was all easily managed. My uncle, retired from the railroad and now wholly engrossed in Bible study, reflected the kind of mildness usually reserved for Victorian novels. He was practically an invisible man, always peering kindly over his wire rimmed glasses and rarely leaving his study. He and my aunt were remarkably fond of each other, and I saw that he had missed her very much.

We brought my bags inside and through a short hallway near the kitchen. There, a doorway opened into my room, a functional space that had been a guest room in its previous life. Walls the color of pale sand almost matched the blonde contemporary furniture. Two benign art prints hung next to each other on a long wall, and light came from a long high window over the bed. A cheery corn flower blue bedspread and pillow shams reminded me in a gentle way that I was not a guest here, and this was a room I could make my very own. When I finished unpacking, my clothes did not nearly fill up the large chest or the closet, which made it seem very tidy and well-kept right from the beginning. It was comfortable and quiet, and I could pile up pillows on the bed and read or do what was about to become my favorite new thing: listening to the latest popular music.

I discovered pretty quickly that the local heart throb, a popular DJ, lived right next door. I met him and his adorable family, and I started tuning in to his radio show. He played all the top popular songs teenagers listened to day and night. Living so close became a plus because the other girls were awestruck that I actually lived next door to him. Frequently they asked me if I could get them his autograph. It seemed a little strange to me at first, but later I felt like an emissary with an important job to do. My neighbor always just smiled when I showed up at his door again, as if he was used to all this adoration.

My aunt gave me a turquoise portable radio to keep on the night stand beside my bed. Most nights, after I was supposed to be asleep, I put it under the covers and listened with the volume turned way down. It was my introduction to the music of my generation. I fell completely in love with Del Shannon and his song, "Runaway." I also had a small crush on Pat Boone, and I adored his recording of "Moody River." There were a lot of happy hours spent with that radio listening to Connie Francis, the Everly Brothers, Elvis, Ricky Nelson and others. Music gave me something in common with the other girls, something I could talk about with my new friends at school. I was surprised by the effect music had on me. Whatever that undefined feeling was, I was steeped in it. It had the same unexplained power as the orange groves, the blue sky and the warm southern California air. As the months passed, the days of music and sunshine blended into a seamless memory that I bottled up. Something in me knew I would probably need it later.

The rooms in my aunt's home were furnished, not with the antiques I had lived with my whole life, but with very contemporary, functional furniture. The dining room table and chairs were a dark, unpretentious walnut. Blinds covered all the windows instead of curtains or drapes, and a large mirror hung on one living room wall. There were no pictures or knick-knacks or anything non-essential, nothing to gather dust that sometimes floated in from the groves. I understood eventually how much this reflected my aunt's approach to decorating, and to life in general.

She was definitely a no-frills kind of woman. I could even say she was all-business, but that wouldn't really be quite accurate. In spite of her sharp ability to immediately size things up and see them for what they were, she possessed a very original sort of kindness. It was soft and easy and led you to believe that your faults, whatever they were, would be immediately forgiven. Here in the happy, uncomplicated rooms of her house, my personal world was entirely held in place by church and school and family. It was an atmosphere that would never, under any circumstances, be subject to change. Sometimes, I wondered if this was an illusion that might shift suddenly, but it never did.

Her home ran with clock-like precision. People and things had a place where they belonged. No untidy areas or discord interrupted the easy, guileless contentment. The atmosphere here was a tangible thing, the music of home that I could take with me now and play anywhere. In my aunt's house, I saw the idea of what home could look like. The rooms were all arranged in the same harmonious way, and there was something enormously peaceful and comforting in that. Years later it became a mental outline for decorating my own home, and in some ways, decorating my own life.

My aunt always sat with me over cups of after-school tea before we started supper, or we read sometimes or I did my homework in the evening while the light slipped away. Those after-school chats had a stabilizing effect. Anything that might have disturbed me melted away in the simplicity of my conversations with her. We sat on bar stools and had all of our meals on the gray formica kitchen counter that my aunt kept impressively shiny and free from any kind of clutter. Her meals were uncomplicated affairs. We ate and talked together and returned the kitchen to its pristine condition when we were finished.

A careful, disciplined woman by nature, my aunt kept all the accounting books for the apartment buildings she and my uncle owned. I sat sometimes watching her write small numbers into the long pages of a ledger book. There were no computers in that era. Everything was written in her neat hand in ink. I thought those pages of neat columns looked very official and impressive, and I wondered if someday I might possibly have my very own ledger book with my own columns of numbers.

My aunt was born in Oklahoma in 1910, during America's hard, early years. She married a local boy in 1929, and they followed their dream of life in the big city, to Chicago. They arrived just in time for the Great Depression. She worked as a waitress among other things, and they both had a series of small jobs at a time when there were thousands of people in bread lines in the streets. I listened to her stories about the hardships of the Depression; how cardboard inside shoes would cover holes worn all the way through, and how ice water could

MY AUNT AND UNCLE

23

bring limp, discarded vegetables back to life. She must have been very industrious even at twenty, because eventually she and my uncle saved enough to make their next move to what was then the golden dreamland of so many, California.

Apparently they did well and invested wisely in real estate, because when I lived with them she was very busy with the apartment buildings they owned. Sometimes when a tenant moved out we would go over to re-plaster and paint. This was my first exposure to maintenance and repair, and I eventually became a pretty good plasterer. I learned to mix the water and plaster, patch holes and blot the surface so that it matched the wall around it. Then, we all sat around on the floor eating bags of hot dripping tacos until we were ready to paint. Paint covered a multitude of sins, making a whole apartment feel fresh and new. It was a revolutionary discovery, the power of a bucket of paint.

My aunt's life was incredibly consistent in every way, including her religious point of view. Having come at middle age to salvation, she and my uncle made a serious commitment to a small church as their spiritual home. Some of the family thought that my aunt and uncle chose this somewhat insignificant little church because it would lead to their more rapid advancement, as though personal ambition was the primary reason for such decisions. This idea seemed fundamentally wrong to me, especially when I thought of the kind ladies with their flannel boards. I suspected that benefits for themselves would not be very high on their list of reasons to give unruly children all those hours of their time.

Even as a child, I knew that goodness, raw kindness, existed. People did things for others all the time that had nothing to do with benefits for themselves. I clung tenaciously to goodwill as a source of comfort within the reach of anyone, to make life better than it might be otherwise. These issues about goodness and the motives for it were my first encounters with points of view that were fundamentally opposed to each other. It was helpful to see these contrasts so early, and living in my aunt's house was a perfect opportunity to discover the things that somehow, had a "rightness" about them.

My aunt and I took trips together to Yosemite or Hesperia down in the valley or shopping in Riverside and Pomona. We went to Knott's Berry Farm ( my favorite), the amusement park in Long Beach and the new attraction, Disneyland. We all camped out sometimes in their travel trailer at Big Bear and caught trout to cook for breakfast on cold mornings over an open fire. The geography of California had no immediate end that I could see. There were palm-lined streets, deserts, immense redwoods, cliffs overlooking Big Sur and lush canyons in Santa Monica. The California of those days was a paradise in every direction just waiting to be discovered.

Sometimes my aunt took me with her on speaking engagements, standard affairs in some town not far away where she had been invited to teach the Bible to some group of church ladies. She always packed in a lot of very well-organized information, and I absorbed it all like a sponge. I got the whole antediluvian and postdiluvian thing down right away and had a pretty good grasp of the major characters. I considered it riveting stuff. I went to conferences with her and met missionaries who made real impressions on me. They had interesting stories to tell, and I always came away from these meetings with two things: a lot of notes and the residual comfort that came from being around some of the best people I would ever meet on this earth.

My aunt's house eventually began to serve another purpose. It became a sort of outpost similar to those used by hardened explorers in some jungle camp at the base of Kilimanjaro. Like a miniature guide charged with forging new trails, I went on my little exploits wearing shorts and my grubby tennis shoes, fearlessly roaming our rustic paradise. There apparently was an emerging adventurer in myself, an impetuous twin that I finally met after a while during my amateur rambles. I wondered if she was more the real me, or if my book reading, tea-drinking self was the real me. I could never actually decide, but I was seriously captivated by the beauty of flowering cacti and the idyllic atmosphere of the groves.

*"I went on my little exploits wearing shorts and my grubby tennis shoes, fearlessly roaming our rustic paradise."*

Always waiting for me there in the late shadows of the afternoon as I walked home from school, the groves became like my friends. I could count on them. They demanded nothing, required nothing from me, but simply stood solid and fine in an impenetrable green splendor. I loved them, and they loved me back. The cool, dense shade heavily scented with the fragrance of orange blossoms and dark, freshly-turned earth was an overpowering invitation to another world. There was one afternoon when I stumbled upon a place in the groves where slanting shafts of sunlight poured down through the branches, bathing everything in extraordinary light. It felt very much like holy ground, and I could see beyond the light into a realm that I can only describe as, invisible. It might as well have been church, the encounter was so similar, with furrowed rows for pews and leafy branches for the walls. I think too, there might have been some angels just there at the edges of the light, keeping watch like they did in the rugged fields of lands far away. It had the completeness of a sanctuary, more so than many of the houses of worship I would ever visit. I felt a kind of salvation in the moments standing there on the plowed ground bathed in the light. It lent itself to my long search for "something." On that day, and other days, I was faintly changed by my quiet explorations in the groves where I felt happier and more secure. They were uncomplicated changes, quiet, easy and I was relieved to discover, permanent.

Fortunately the environment of my aunt's home was entirely favorable to my little journeys into the groves, and every discovery complimented everything that had happened before it. There were other discoveries too, other "firsts" in my young life. I had never ridden in cars with boys, and our church youth group gave me my very first exposure to that kind of exhilaration. After prayer meetings sometimes, all the teenagers piled into two cars driven by the high school boys, and we went out for milk shakes at some local drive-in. This seemed like very grown up stuff to me, and I started to imagine what it would be like to actually go out alone with a boy on a date. The idea was incredibly romantic. Lying in bed at night I spent a lot of time thinking about what cute boy might ask me out, what I would wear and what we might talk about.

I started paying attention to the older girls, what they wore and how they did their hair. I saw right away they were all way ahead of me in several respects. For one thing they were all permanently golden as people are who have lived in paradise forever. The idea of tanning was new to me, but I started sitting out on our back patio surrounded by the tall red cannas, and gradually my Oklahoma skin looked less pale. I hoped, once the sun had worked its magic, I would look like the nonchalantly golden girls with the sun bleached, windswept hair usually associated with surf boards and convertibles. They were associated too, with very tall, equally blond and hopelessly attractive boys one sees only in California. There were quite a few obvious reasons why California was called the Golden State.

My aunt made a whole new life possible for me and gave me a world of things to experience for the very first time: the train ride, my exposure to music, the joys of tea, exploring Big Bear and the California coast. She introduced me to the groves and the world beyond them. All of these things were mine now, permanent gifts from her with lasting benefits that changed the direction of my life. We had hours to chat when she and I traveled together, and we talked sometimes like grown ups do, about important things, about the future. She encouraged me to go to college, to be a serious student, and I really did not want to ever disappoint her. We understood each other in a way that was just an easy thing, and living in her house gave us a past to draw on that would always be there. In all the years later that separated us, I never felt she was very far away.

I didn't think ahead to the days when my stay with her would be over. I thought that maybe this might last a long time. My parents were worlds away, and I had no idea of what their circumstances were. Eventually though, there were phone calls. There were plans to come and retrieve me. I did miss my father, and like always, I hoped that this would be the beginning of something new, something better. It just seemed too soon when all the months of my life with my aunt and the days in the dependable groves were over.

My parents drove out to pick me up and stayed to visit a few days before we started back. I sat mostly quiet, listening to the kind of aimless conversations people have when they are already thinking of being somewhere else.

I remember my aunt's face and our last goodbye. It was really not a hard thing, not like an end of anything. It just seemed like a normal place in the path of our lives together. I had my packed bags waiting there by the door, and I smoothed over the corn flower blue bedspread one more time. I walked over to give her a last hug, and we both smiled at each other, just like always. She stood casually on the front porch when it was time for my parents to pull away. She had on that pretty gray skirt and the silky pink blouse that she wore to meetings sometimes, and she said goodbye with a cheery wave as if I was just leaving for a church picnic. If she knew our eventual destination, she did not seem alarmed by it. She was never actually alarmed by anything. In her customary, confident manner, she believed I would be all right. And, I was.

## Chapter 3

# THE QUARTER

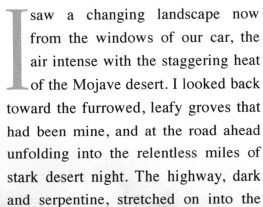

I saw a changing landscape now from the windows of our car, the air intense with the staggering heat of the Mojave desert. I looked back toward the furrowed, leafy groves that had been mine, and at the road ahead unfolding into the relentless miles of stark desert night. The highway, dark and serpentine, stretched on into the

next small bits of a future where, against my will, California began to recede, little by little. The images were not quite as sharp, but it had still done its work, made its impression. In its place were new currents that carried me along in a river of transition, winding through remarkably forgettable stopping places and unmemorable pauses, days and weeks I just wanted to forget. The new currents left a long rolling wake behind them in the violent red sunsets, like a curtain coming down on a play that would never be performed again.

I felt like the member of a reluctant audience who were forced at last to rise from our seats and abandon the appealing atmosphere of the imaginary theater for the cold, uninviting sidewalks outside. To me, the gray streets and houses sitting beyond the bright security of the theater seemed like such merciless things, devoid of sanctuary and imagination. The curtain had gone down now, and nothing would ever be this wonderful, this grand again. There is always that

little shock after a performance when the house lights come up and the flash of disappointment appears. It is our reminder that it was only a play, that we must leave the known comforts of the theater and go home now. That illusion, that regret, lasted all the long days and miles in front of me.

Traveling through a swirling world of change, I couldn't quite see where I had been or where I was going. There was a dull, indefinable sameness in the next days and weeks, dissolving into a gradual blur. I noticed later how much of life is like that; hours punctuated only by being present and waiting for something, waiting for the next place to open. My own next place was waiting somewhere. Only the currents of life knew where. There were no dangerous rapids to navigate thankfully, only indolent waters moving me along, a captive of some hidden rhythm. My images of California slowly became less distinct. A vagueness attached itself to each tiny moment, diminishing the vibrance that had been there just yesterday. But then I remembered, I was rich now, permanently wealthy, a beneficiary of the opportunity and security the California days gave me, and I brought every one of those assets with me.

Lulled by some odd sense of detachment and my senses deadened by sleep, I felt the arrival in our new place rather than seeing it. I think it took me days to see it. It was a dreamlike state that appeared to be real and not real all at the same time. I had drifted far beyond my safe moorings in the west and landed in a place that offered something excessively new. There were bricks under my feet, long shutters on sweeping, ornate galleries above, and the faint smell of the city. We had arrived somewhere. The determined currents of life deposited me in probably the unlikeliest of places in the summer of 1962, the Vieux Carré, the French Quarter of New Orleans.

It was a flamboyantly earthy world, as if a divine alchemist had poured some exotic potion into the atmosphere. Evidence of a rampant joie de vivre spilled out in profusion everywhere, transforming the landscape of the Quarter into an aesthetically ornamental place. Permanently locked in the embrace of its lover, the Mississippi

River, and anchored by intermediate blocks of a relatively small world, it was as unlike California, my former sedate and leafy world, as it could possibly be. The streets were constantly crowded, full of the exuberant people who lived here or wished they could live here. Summer had overtaken the city and Bourbon Street was alive with throngs eager to experience the gaudy strip clubs, bars and iridescent nightlife. I heard it mentioned a few times as a decadent world full of enticing vices and wickedly intoxicating beverages. I viewed it though, through the eyes of an innocent. I hadn't learned yet, the art of finding flaws in everything and everyone.

My father had family there. His artist brother lived in one of the many courtyard apartments behind the iron gates dotting every street. The Quarter seemed to be a safe haven of sorts while my father looked for a job and made another brave attempt at forging a new family path for us. He would not succeed entirely. He did eventually find a job, but his plans for the new family path would be as illusive and unattainable as ever.

We finally finished unpacking in the dull heat of our apartment, the windows flung wide open to the humid, breathless air of the Quarter, and I began to feel the first, faint sensations of adjustment. It was slow in coming because this atmosphere was so deliberately unhurried. Eventually, in the first unsteady days, among the ruins of the most recent family discord, an idea began to form in my mind. I began to think about becoming a nun. It seemed like a peaceful life. It might not be filled with too many problems, and I could be quietly invisible there. I discarded this notion pretty quickly after honestly evaluating my virtues and realizing they were insufficient for such a serious vocation. I had actually thought about it before. The seeds of holiness were firmly planted by my aunt who, though not Catholic, still encouraged me to think about God in a serious way. Part of me yearned for the uninterrupted simplicity of a convent, and nuns just seemed like very nice people.

A few days into our arrival in the Quarter I began my explorations in the most obvious place, Jackson Square. In my lace head covering, I knelt quietly there in the St. Louis Cathedral in the French Quarter of New Orleans and resolved to be good. I wanted to excel at something and goodness seemed like a worthy and possibly attainable goal. The elevated ideals of sainthood appealed to me, and it was remarkably easy to feel holy here. The Cathedral was grand inside, cavernous and dark, a worthy destination for seekers, the penitent and the distressed. Conveniently, I was all three. I longed for eternity, grieved over my sins and lamented the sorry state of the world as only a fifteen-year-old can. I went sometimes to early mass and many afternoons lit a candle and fervently prayed for my soul and the souls of those already departed. They seemed in my young mind to be still with me, and maybe they were.

*"The elevated ideals of sainthood appealed to me, and it was remarkably easy to feel holy here."*

I decided to become a nun partly too, because the environment of the French Quarter lent itself so perfectly to this idea. The atmosphere was entirely different from the simplicity of my previously golden days in California. Surrounded by bohemian artists, exotic dancers, itinerant musicians, tormented authors and the sometimes inebriated, it was not difficult to see where the general line between the good and the less good might be drawn. But I was not uncomfortable with any of these people, and I simply thought of them as neighbors since I saw them frequently on the street or getting coffee or kneeling in earnest prayer a few seats over from me in the St. Louis Cathedral. I was so intent during those days on the idea of life in the convent that it was a bit disconcerting to discover, weeks later, that perhaps I had been a little reckless in my intentions. I was already seeing life now through a newer lens, and everything had changed completely.

The narrow streets forming the Quarter were a compact space nestled against the river and downtown, and as the days passed, exploring with the rest of the tourists, I started to feel at home. The Quarter was defined by a few specific things: the Mississippi River, the Cathedral in Jackson Square, the Café du Monde, Bourbon Street, the music that drifted from Preservation Hall and art. There was lots of art. The streets were full of artists busy with paints and brushes. Canvases exploding with color filled the walls of countless galleries. It all seemed terribly original. There was a creative energy here. It mixed with the oils and pastels in a kind of liquid emotion that expressed itself in the images of the Quarter. Historic scenery, courtyards and streets, buildings and wrought iron, ferns and great palms bent low in the shadows of afternoon light all begged to be immortalized on canvas, and every artist accommodated them. It was like a living art museum, its existence daily multiplied by the hands of the faithful who lived and painted here, as though there was no other place on earth but this place.

Fortunately, the apartment occupied by my uncle was just beyond the corner of Bourbon and St. Peter in the block across from Pat O'Brien's and Preservation Hall. It was the most perfect place imaginable to see and hear the throngs of people crowding the sidewalks of the Quarter at all hours. They came by the thousands. Some came for the music and jazz clubs like Pete Fountain's just around the corner. I joined them in Preservation Hall sometimes, sitting in the unsteady wooden chairs scattered in irregular rows against the decaying walls while we waited for the musicians to begin playing the next round of Dixieland jazz. I remember the piano and the clarinet most and the cascading harmonies coaxed out of them entirely without sheet music. It just came uncontrived from somewhere deep within the souls of these men, seductively floating out on the night air of the Quarter like an immortal signature of heavenly notes.

Beyond the music, the famed food and drink of the Quarter drew flocks of supplicants, those who came to eat at places like the Court of Two Sisters, Brennan's, Galatoire's or Arnaud's. There were daily or sometimes hourly detailed discussions about where one had eaten or was planning to eat, and what precisely had been or would be consumed and with whom. A revolving merry-go-round, the Carousel Bar of the Monteleone Hotel overlooking Royal Street (a place I desperately wanted to go) had an endlessly enthusiastic parade of guests spilling joyfully out onto the sidewalk before moving on, drifting further into the Quarter to their next appointment in an evening of exotic libations.

Occupying the same densely crowded sidewalks were other endlessly ardent lovers of the night, moving to the same music that permeated the darkness. They were the ones who came to drink, party and enjoy the sensual pleasures of the clubs lining the blocks along Bourbon Street. Among the throngs, taken all together in one sweeping glance, there was a collective thirst for exhilaration, however temporary it might be. Within the boundaries of the streets, restaurants and clubs was a kind of pleasing communal and complicit détente that accommodated and made room for everyone who came here in search of something. Some who came were the quieter types, the visitors who came for the history or just for a "taste" of the famous Quarter. I saw them sometimes walking slowly, glancing at a map and then at the street signs, taking everything in. The Quarter has a "feel" to it. These quiet ones and others, too, came for that.

When I went to breakfast sometimes at the Bourbon House just on the corner, it was always quiet in the early morning. Bourbon Street as far up as I could see and St. Peter, too, were entirely still. I looked up at the old brick buildings with their wrought iron balconies and thought of all the people still fast asleep and in no particular hurry to grapple with the difficulties of morning. People tended to sleep late. No one rushed about here. This laissez faire atmosphere was as consistent and as silent as the sunrise. I roamed the streets of the Quarter entirely and safely alone at all hours, as everyone did who lived here.

The streets around the Cathedral stayed busy, full of visitors exploring the Cabildo or the French Market. I wove my way among them, making my daily pilgrimage to Café du Monde for beignets and my first encounters with café au lait, laced with chicory. Sitting there in the morning light at my round table looking out on Decatur Street, I discovered that the powdered sugar from the beignets simply went everywhere. It was impossible to restrain it in any way as every breath disturbed it. The first lesson was not to inhale when taking a bite, but even then the white powder took flight often in the slightest breeze leaving an embarrassing trail behind it. It was obvious after a while who had been having their morning beignets because frequently they were wearing the evidence.

The food of New Orleans was an unanticipated discovery, and probably changed my life as much as the dining car. Breakfast, lunch and dinner were educational opportunities. I was a hopelessly addicted seafood lover now, and the prospect of what to eat next was impossibly exciting. The invention of the legendary po-boy was responsible for possibly many of my happiest hours. New Orleans French bread was piled high with fried shrimp or fried oysters, soft shell crabs, crawfish, roast beef or some other delectable meat and served dressed or undressed. I preferred mine dressed, topped with shredded slaw or lettuce. My first exposure to them happened in those small establishments with dark interiors, brick walls and floors the color of ancient tobacco. They occupied the side streets usually unknown to the tourists and their kitchens turned out oyster po-boys, fat muffulettas stuffed with Italian meats and olive salad, jambalaya, and steaming hot platters of crabs and fish from the Gulf. Eating at places like this changed how I thought and felt about food.

Gumbo, the darkest I ever saw, almost black and full of thick shrimp, became one of the great comforts of my life. It came with a scoop of steaming white rice and hot French bread slathered with butter. Everyone said that gumbo originated in New Orleans. The roux was the primary thing, and the secret was getting it just dark enough without burning. There was always something extraordinarily soothing to me about a big pot of gumbo simmering on the stove. I started experimenting with it later on when I was brave enough to attempt cooking new things, and I added andouille sausage and blue crabs with their big whole claws that we all broke apart with our hands and ate like pirates.

*"The unmistakable smell of fried shrimp, hot with hushpuppies... almost brought me to my knees sometimes."*

The unmistakable smell of fried shrimp, hot with hushpuppies right out of the deep fryer almost brought me to my knees sometimes. It drifted out onto the sidewalks from those little places with the dark interiors where heavy platters came out piled high with the French fries, shrimp and hushpuppies, begging to be eaten without a fork. I wondered how many hungry people sat there at those worn counters in happy oblivion, up to their elbows in this greasy, crunchy heaven.

Breakfast could be surprising too, and I discovered grits dripping in butter. But, it was the eggs Sardou and eggs Benedict that made me fall in love with brunch as an almost religious experience. I really warmed to the idea that a person could be rewarded for sleeping late. Here, the rewards were things like poached eggs and hollandaise topped with lump crab meat, and dessert crepes floating in a delectable sauce of caramelized sugar, cognac and orange peel. These were rewards that I could get used to. Later in life I added champagne and found that brunch could make up for quite a few things that might have otherwise led to a bad day. Breakfast in the Quarter could just sometimes be a simple platter of softly scrambled eggs and sausage and real New Orleans French bread spread with so much butter that I needed my own cow, but it would never be, could never be ordinary.

Dinner on certain occasions was a spectacular business when someone pointed me toward little bites of heaven like oysters Bienville, shrimp remoulade, crabmeat imperial, and coquilles St. Jacques, iconic culinary classics all famous for their place in the food history here. They were served as they had been for decades in the dining rooms of historic restaurants like Antoine's which had been here for over a century. It was impossible to go there, to sit in the atmosphere and not feel a sense of history. The bays, shallow bayous, lakes and rivers all around New Orleans were full of red fish, flounder, speckled trout, crawfish and scallops that wound up at dinner as etouffée, crawfish Napoleon with ravigote sauce or trout Pontchartrain, among others. The impressions of that food, all those formidable meals, are one of the things I remember most about that summer in the Quarter.

I started very soon to feel the subtle magic the Quarter exerts over those who merely walk along its streets. The confluence of old and older, infinitely charming courtyards hidden behind the ornate iron gates and scents hanging heavy in the warm air, all conspired together to create a numbing anesthetic. It simply melted away whatever bad thing that might have inserted itself into the day.

The Mississippi River lazily winding through the city had that kind of power, too. Its effect on the atmosphere seemed both wild and restrained all at the same time, as if at any moment it might of its own accord, choose to rise again. Shifting colors and steady currents defined the winding riverfront, and the influences of the river reached far beyond its banks to the green boundaries of leafy parks with ancient twisting oaks. The moss draped oaks were silent, green sentinels reflecting the early days when countless duels were famously fought in New Orleans, interrupting the aspirations of the living in a profitable world defined by the river.

I looked out over the water from my bench on the wharf, watching the insistent momentum in the center swift and relentless, while the small eddies at the edges came in circles sometimes drifting upstream. I had seen the raw power of the river before from the bridge at Vicksburg, the brown and ominous torrent raging below, hurling itself against the levees carrying huge fallen trees and debris with it. When it flooded, like it did in the great flood of 1927, the whole Delta felt it, and nothing was safe along the miles of weakened levees as the muddy waters spilled out violently in all directions. But it was not that way now on the placid waterfront of the Quarter. Its fierce inclinations were slumbering and untroubled in its steady flow south toward the Gulf. There was a vague, primal quality in the gray waves that rippled across the surface. It was not hard to imagine why riverboat captains of the past had been so captivated by those powerful, rolling currents. Those turbulent waters of the Mississippi were an invitation to a whole wide world that existed all by itself.

The river and a thousand other things made their contributions to the layers of life in the Quarter. It was, in its purest form, a small village, grand in scope, but still reflecting the innate qualities of the people who called it home. Many of the writers and artists had a predictably eccentric flair for life unburdened by provincialism. They were followed closely by the musicians who played on and on into the endless nights. I met one of them who had an extravagant amount of joy. He was a magician with the clarinet, coaxing sounds from the depths of his soul. He also apparently had a gift for superior red beans and rice. He would never tell me his closely guarded secret, but he actually gave me a few hints about making it. I suspected that he made red beans and rice with the same passion that he played the clarinet. It was a unique thing, being so surrounded by art in every form that was alive and unburdened by whatever conventions that might have preceded them.

My uncle, the artist, began to take me around with him to the galleries on Royal Street where he had his paintings. The conversations there were the kind that artists always had, and being with him made me feel very grown up. He was a handsome man, tall and quiet with flowing white hair and a smile that was kind. Everything about him suggested a beautiful, quiet strength and a patient soul full of remarkable warmth and generosity. He painted landscapes of the buildings and courtyards of the Quarter in oils, though I did see an occasional pastel. He was always impeccably dressed and had one or two paintings under one arm when we went on a circuit of the galleries. His work was really quite good and I watched him some afternoons in Pirate's Alley painting with the

THE COURT OF TWO SISTERS

other artists. We went occasionally on other excursions, walking the long blocks of Royal Street past the galleries and antique shops all the way to Canal Street.

In Maison Blanche, the superb department store that dominated Canal Street, my uncle managed to give me the impression that there was simply nothing else in the world he would rather do than wander about a department store with an excitable young girl gripped in the budding stages of a shopping addiction. There was a small diner near a corner on Canal where we sat sometimes while I ate melted cheese sandwiches and listened to him talk in his low quiet voice about art. These were the easiest moments, when learning happened without any sort of effort, and I felt as if I had known him my whole life.

He had friends who discussed writing and books. I heard famous names like Tennessee Williams, Frances Parkinson Keyes and William Faulkner who at one time or another, had all lived

45

here. I walked by the Beauregard-Keyes house on Chartres Street sometimes, and it was strange to think of her actually living right there in that house and writing those novels about New Orleans society. Her books were my introduction to the grand detail and interesting characters of the historical novel. There was a vast amount of literary history associated with the Carousel Bar at the Monteleone. Evidently Tennessee Williams, the celebrated playwright spent a lot of time sitting in those embellished seats that moved in slow circles, and so did other authors like Ernest Hemingway and Truman Capote.

For me, all the weeks in this heady labyrinth of riches was an education without a classroom. Without desks or homework, it was a laboratory of sorts, like a living experiment. As the student, I took away knowledge, but none of it was contained in books. It came primarily from people, transparent moments and passing conversations like one I had with an ancient lady in the French Market one day. I bought two almost warm pralines from her, wrapped in paper. She wore a faded blue dress. Her eyes were the cloudy gray of the sea and behind them were years and years of living. She was a person I would remember. I had other small exchanges too, inadvertent encounters with uncommon personalities in the fertile environment of the Quarter that affected and changed me. My impressions of small incidents like that drifted indistinctly in my subconscious a little like ghosts, but the memory of them stayed close to me, near enough to be remembered.

Later, after my father moved us around the long curve of the Gulf to the Mississippi coast, I came on the train to visit the Quarter at Mardi Gras. Other times I came over with friends to Audubon Park, Lake Pontchartrain or shopping on Canal Street. But always, I thought of the French Quarter with real fondness as my second home. It had three images, and in my mind they never changed; I always saw my uncle with his flowing white hair, a painting under his arm. I saw the Cafe du Monde, me sitting there with a plate of steaming beignets, and I saw the Cathedral, a refuge with the supernatural power to anchor souls, or at least steady them. I would always come here. When I sat in the cool dimness of the Cathedral or across the square at the cafe, I saw my uncle's face, and I remembered those days. I thought of those streets, the aroma of gumbo and fried oyster po-boys, artist brushes that smelled of oil paint and turpentine, Dixieland jazz that played all night and hot, sticky air off the river scented with mud and catfish. Those things were part of me now, and I was part of them. It was a picture that, for one finite moment, had me in it. My aunt was right not to be worried about me. I had been just as safe, just as cared for, in the galleried streets of the French Quarter of New Orleans as I had been in the comfortable bedroom with the corn flower blue bedspread in her house among the orange groves.

## Chapter 4

# THE COAST

Late in the summer, the familiar streets of the Quarter changed, an almost imperceptible shift. Contently drifting in the easy laissez faire, I didn't see it coming. But it was characteristic of the enigmatic life familiar to me now. One of the chief advantages of living life on a perpetual vacation is the illusion that it will continue indefinitely. The burdens of planning, of decisions, are pushed far out into the remote borders of consciousness until it is easy to forget about them entirely. When I came up the steps of our apartment one morning and found my parents packing, it was an abrupt reminder of some realities I had ignored for these past weeks. My father simply said, smiling, that we were all going to the beach, to the Mississippi coast, somewhere I had never been. And just like that, as the doors of New Orleans closed for me, the doors of Mississippi swung wide open.

My father was the slender thread that held our unsettled family unit together. In our most recent adversity he had decided to put down our remaining tenuous roots in a place where I could start and finish high school without moving again. I understood his decision later when we sat on a white beach and talked about it. It was another new beginning. We said our goodbyes and promised future visits. Then we loaded the car, left our apartment in the Quarter behind and drove away into the full sun of a summer day. We rode along in a small breeze, the windows of our un-air-conditioned gray Buick down, hoping to dull the effects of the humid air of the city. We left Canal Street behind with its clanging street cars and people crowding the sidewalks. I wanted to wave to them out the window, to say goodbye to these strangers, to remind them I was going away. I was leaving, again.

We went east on the Chef Menteur Highway, Highway 90 that took us through miles of water and marsh past White Kitchen and across the Pearl River Bridge into Hancock County, Mississippi. Wild marshlands, miles of foreign vegetation in alternating shades of green merged with escaping swamp water running through them in long meandering fingers. An untroubled ease permeated the atmosphere everywhere here, separated by invisible borders from the world outside. It had an unmistakable quality about it, a feeling of identifiable warmth that defined Mississippi as much as the green marsh and bayous. I came to Mississippi full of vague hopes, and right away, this overpowering pleasantness attached itself to me until I was eventually, and agreeably, lost in it.

Not far away were the blue waters of the Gulf, a place I had never been, never seen. These same waters had been the landing place of the French in 1699 newly-come in the name of King Louis XIV to claim Biloxi, the first settlement of French Louisiana. Romantic sounding names like Pierre Le Moyne d'Iberville, his brother Bienville, the pirate Jean Lafitte and others, the explorers and settlers, still lived here. They resided on the coast in history books and in graveyards centuries old. I had a faint impression from the very first that ghostlike versions of them might still be at home out on the barrier islands of the Mississippi Sound or camped among the inland thickets, still claiming the lands in the name of France.

We drove east until the world began to change into something bigger, like a doorway to impossibly white sand covered beaches. Crossing finally over the bridge at Bay St. Louis, the blue Gulf appeared right in front of me, and I saw it for the first time. Out on the horizon were hints of land, Cat Island and Ship Island, but they were larger in my imagination. I wondered if people went out there in boats, like an adventure on the long rolling waves.

Every advancing mile along the white beach filled me with more excitement. It was the ocean, the Gulf of Mexico, and I couldn't wait to fling myself into it. Highway 90 took us on along the beach through Pass Christian, Long Beach and Gulfport to Mississippi City. I never knew why my father decided to stop there, but he did, and we checked into the white stucco Alamo Plaza that sat facing the Gulf. This was our summer holiday, and after a week at the motel we rented one of the small gray summer cottages next door on a street called Venetian Gardens with a view of the beach.

Moss-hung oaks lined a beachfront with the whitest sand I had ever seen. Through the open windows of our summer cottage I heard the first dull sounds of waves hitting the beach and smelled the warm breeze saturated with salt air. It was a variegated landscape ripened by years, and it managed to be subtle and overpowering all at the same time. California and the French Quarter had been places I loved for all kinds of reasons, but it was here on the Coast that I became more myself than I would ever be anywhere else. To say that these thoughts first came to me there on that stretch of sand would not be entirely true because I felt it, the effect of the place, as we crossed the bridge at Bay St. Louis, the blue Gulf stretched out in front of me. It might have even been before that, an intangible moment on Mississippi soil, breathing Mississippi air. I thought later that it knew me before I knew "it," and it had always been here, waiting for me to arrive.

> *"It was the ocean, the Gulf of Mexico, and I couldn't wait to fling myself into it."*

So much has been written about this place from the perspectives of others and their own experiences here, from their own thoughts on what meanings Mississippi has, and has had. The moonlight, magnolias and moss-covered oaks have been often bathed in criticism as clichéd cultural relics, as if somehow, even their diminutive green

53

leaves must be summoned to repentance. I could never think of them that way. Bound as I must be to my own authentic past and my expression of it, it would be correct to say that I felt the benevolent embrace of the moss-covered oaks even before I got here, long before. And now, tangled in their misty, gray-green blankets, they were here to welcome me home. They were, among all the other idyllic elements in this cordial atmosphere, a kind of gift. Of all the many places I had been, God had saved this gift for last. I saw Mississippi this way, through fifteen-year-old eyes then, as sympathetic ground, welcoming and gracious. It would not be possible in all the long years ahead for me to think of it any other way.

The regions, the pockets of the South, swing in broad strokes, slashing through pine forests, rolling hills, mountains and miles of rich flat land made for cotton. There are vast differences among them, but a haunting sameness, too. I always felt it most when I crossed the Mississippi River. There was a palpable sense of arrival. The South announced itself in a thousand ways, and it certainly did on the Gulf Coast. A long expanse of gracious old waterfront homes extended almost unbroken from Pass Christian through Gulfport to

Biloxi. Built largely from local pine and cypress, many of them were the summer homes of people from New Orleans, or they were used for entire households to escape the yellow fever epidemics. These elegant homes in the shade of large oaks facing the Gulf all had uniquely different and charming architectural styles, and I thought there was something reassuring about their endurance and tenacity.

After a while, I saw the Coast went beyond the white beach filled with tourists. It was a place of strong impressions, a living history of aging lighthouses, sailors, soldiers and explorers who anchored out at Ship Island because it was the only deep water port between the Mississippi River and Mobile Bay. People left places far away and came here to start new lives and work the lumber mills, railroads and seafood canneries and to fish the waters of the Gulf. Their graves were reminders that they struggled to make this place, and their descendants were still here on this crescent of coast people called the "Riviera of the South." Live oaks, historic homes and churches, imposing hotels and restaurants lined the long curving miles along the blue Gulf. In all the years I lived here, it never stopped being the perfect thing that it was.

Our small cottage was very close to being sublime, and eventually I started to see a picture of what life could be like here. Sitting alone on the white beach, insulated from discord, I eased into the safety of pretending. I always did this everywhere I went. I began pretending that I lived here, had always lived here, and these total strangers were my friends since childhood. This fantasy gave me an immediate sense of belonging here on the Mississippi Gulf Coast where I believed we would be for the next three years. It gave me a head start on the feeling of home that I always hoped would become real after a while.

This short stretch of Highway 90 service road where we lived was essentially a very small world. A short walk took me to all the attractions. The golf course, a thing of lush beauty then called the Broadwater Sea Course, sat at one end of this paradise. The Friendship House, a restaurant, was at the other. In between were the white plaster walls of the Alamo Plaza Motel with its perfect pool. Next door was the long courtyard of the Colonial Cottages and Confederate Inn restaurant. A little further down on Dubuys Road just behind the Friendship House was the real center of entertainment. Exuberant families and children crowded into the Deer Ranch and Six Gun Junction. There were wild, daily shoot-outs in the reproduction frontier town, and can-can girls performed in packed-out shows at the Red Dog Saloon. It was a thoroughly effervescent atmosphere of non-stop entertainment, and people loved every minute of it.

Across Highway 90 on the beach, a long pier extended far out into the water, always dotted day and night with fishermen and people crabbing. They lowered round baskets baited with chicken necks down into the water and then brought them back up loaded with angry and uncooperative blue crabs. These were then dumped

into a bucket to be hauled home for dinner. Sometimes an irritated crustacean deprived of the last chicken neck bolted, escaping in an evil mood and scattering the bare feet around him in all directions. If no one interfered with his hostile retreat down the pier's gray boards, his defiance was sometimes rewarded, and he slipped over the edge to the safety of the shallow waters below. Watching these belligerent escapes could sometimes be very entertaining and my own bare feet had a few close encounters with those aggressive crab pincers. It was surprising the amount of pain they could inflict on unsuspecting toes.

At night, in the distance, a procession of intermittent, bright single lights appeared above the shallows along the beach, people floundering with sharp long gigs in search of the tell-tale shape of a flounder outlined just underneath the surface of the water. Animated children scrambled up and down the sand in the nightly pastime of catching lightning-fast crabs with small nets or their bare hands. Their flashlights blinked off and on in the dark everywhere in the dizzying patterns of energized children. A flashlight disappeared sometimes, lost among the miniature waves and leaving the owner at the mercy of his intended victims. Very quickly though, a procession of other lights came to his rescue, forming once again their formidable force of small figures advancing in the night. The number of crabs caught was hotly contested, and after the counting determined who caught the most, the proud winners were announced. The crabs were then returned to the sea, released from their tiny, sand pail prisons into the shifting tides where undoubtedly they would be recaptured the next night, and all the nights in the immediate future. I was amazed that on this beach, there seemed to be an endless supply of fish and crabs everywhere, mere yards away, waiting to be caught and immediately consumed.

There were other delectable meals here, too, just waiting to be consumed. Family kitchens, restaurants and sometimes deteriorating gas stations continually served hungry people the daily food of the South: fried chicken, grits, collards, spoon bread, hot biscuits, gumbo, fried oysters, shrimp, catfish, tomatoes right out of the garden, homemade pickles and often, someone's mayhaw jelly. Plates and platters piled with seafood fed an army of locals and tourists at restaurants on the water overlooking the Gulf. Fried shrimp, fish, crab cakes, hushpuppies and French fries filled what some restaurants called a "Captain's Platter." This essentially, became my favorite thing, and I think I could have been happy just ordering that forever. All along the Coast, and actually all over Mississippi, was this expansive menu that seemed specifically designed to produce contentment. It was wildly successful at producing quite a bit more than that. It was capable of almost holy moments at someone's kitchen table.

Very few things in life were more satisfying than sitting in someone's warm, unpretentious kitchen with countertops worn down by long years of food and conversation. We might have okra and tomatoes picked that morning or biscuits just out of the oven. There might be chess or lemon pie with golden meringue a mile high on it. Maybe chicken and dumplings sat in a big pot warming on the stove or we ate cold pea salad left over from yesterday. Whatever we had to eat would have a history decades long, and there was more than just comfort in it. I spent time in the kitchen with generous women who made that food every day and twice that much on Sunday. They kept the ones they loved warmed and filled. There would always be big jars of fresh cut cantaloupe in the refrigerator for little children to reach in and grab with their chubby hands or a fresh pot of coffee on the stove to give to somebody that just needed it. Encouragement, hope, friendship and affection all lived in those kitchens along with the comfort that had been born there long decades ago. Its affect on me was remarkable, and I discovered that those meals simply made me feel better, more ready to face whatever troubles clung to life around me. There was an inordinate peace attached to it, and I had never experienced the joyfully liberating effects of Southern food until I came here.

*"...few things in life were more satisfying than sitting in someone's warm, unpretentious kitchen with countertops worn down by long years of food and conversation."*

———— ⋅⋅ ————

The beach was crowded that summer. Half of Mississippi must have been here, the beach blankets, picnic coolers and inflatable rafts of every color bright against the hot white sand. The restaurant tables spilled over with family and extended family, cousins, uncles and aunts, friends, children and teenagers like myself. The beach had really remarkable powers, amazing transformative powers that rendered everyone, including myself, friendly and congenial in a way I had not seen before. We all strolled the beach in a pleasant, unbroken parade along sand wet at the edges from the small frothy waves, lost in the pleasure of walking without having to actually go anywhere or be anywhere. This became my new favorite pastime, that or stretching out on my beach towel baking for hours in the sun, toasting myself to the desired doneness.

Football, I discovered, was revered here. No conversation seemed complete without some reference to teams from towns all over Mississippi. Men had an encyclopedic knowledge of statistics for quarterbacks, running backs and wide receivers that spanned decades. Everyone remembered winning touchdowns and the heroes who made them. Sitting on the beach listening to recollections of the games, I remember being impressed by their vivid descriptions. These were enthusiastic summer people, pleased at the prospect of talking about Mississippi football with someone who was hearing it all for the first time.

Pretty soon, too soon, the tourists gathered the last of the reluctant stragglers from the beach. They piled their station wagons full of bags, souvenirs and happily tired, sunburned people and drove slowly north in the long string of cars on Highway 49 toward Hattiesburg. I met quite a few fellow guests in the long sunny days on the beach and made friends with some of them. They were very friendly girls and boys from high schools in towns like Greenville up in the Delta or Jackson or Starkville. They had happy lives to go back to and were all full of talk now about going back to school and cars and parties and football games. I actually saw some of them again when Gulfport played one of their teams or at summer band camp at the University of Southern Mississippi in Hattiesburg.

It was easy to see why people were always reluctant to leave, to say goodbye to this irresistible place. I could see it as they began gathering

AT THE GULF

things to leave or at their last meal sitting in the Friendship House looking out at the Gulf for the last time. I could see those little traces of sadness in their faces, and I was glad, so very glad to be staying. My father had managed somehow to plant us right in the middle of maybe the most perfect place on the Coast. People thronged to it, clinging to this pretty world for a week or two. But I lived here! It took me a while to actually adjust to the idea. I wasn't packing. I wasn't leaving. I lived here.

## CHAPTER 5

# THE ARMS OF THE GULF

Long sunny days clinging to the blue edges of the Gulf eventually surrendered and made room for something new. My 1962 summer receded in the effortless way it does on the Coast, dragging me slowly and reluctantly along with it. The first hints of fall came with white sand that was not quite as warm against my bare feet and coolness in the salt breeze. The sun set earlier now out on the horizon in more restrained evening displays of pink and gray.

This was what transition looked like. One more season slowly ebbed away, taking the warmth and excitement of an endless summer with it. Even the trees became subdued versions of themselves as if they were embracing winter plans that had already been made. There were plans made for me, too, and like the trees, I was already becoming a new version of myself.

Gulfport High School, a vintage, red brick building constructed in 1923, filled an entire corner of 15th Street comfortably near the beach. Double front doors above wide concrete steps opened to rambling hallways of dark wood floors and broad, creaking stairs to the second floor. Stepping inside the walls was stepping into history, right at forty years of it. Tall glass cases of shining trophies and photographs of distinguished faces lined the front hall, conspicuous reminders of glorious victories. I stood there looking at it all for the first time when I went to register as a new student. It made me feel slightly more important, being in a place so obviously impressive. I had new classes, new books, new teachers, new everything and I was already thinking about pep rallies and football games, choir practice and what clubs to join. I hoped, once I got past the first uneasy weeks, after I learned where all my classes were and made a few friends, I would begin to feel like I belonged here.

Immediately, before any happy future could even begin, I had to face the dreaded first day of school. That was the morning I walked into a classroom completely alone with no small talk to hide behind, no friend to smile at casually as if we had done this a million times. Ordinarily this was only a small challenge for which I had some acquired skills. I already had some experience with "first days." But now I had some disturbing flashbacks, memories of an unsavory past, my dreary, brown plaid and puffed sleeve past. The harder I tried to forget this early episode, the more it attached itself to my mind. It was relentless. I might just be sitting idly on the beach, a typical day in the sunshine where everything was all golden and perfect, thinking about what to wear on the first day of school. Then it would happen, a spiraling descent into the murky waters of despair. I think it was triggered actually by accessories, innocent things usually, but it all began with the shoes.

I knew, like many others, that the wrong shoes just totally wreck an otherwise perfect outfit. To me, the shoe world was and still is a fairy land of endless reasons to be excited, much like a box of chocolates with clandestine centers waiting to be discovered. Shoes exuded style. They possessed color. Buying new shoes was a day brightener guaranteed, unless someone completely ignored both color and style and chose shoes purely for utility and long wear. Think "ugly." This is what happened to me. When I was six, for my first grade school shoes, I got stuck with a pair of saddle oxfords, not the attractive kind with the light, slender soles. Mine were the other kind, the ones with the clunky, extra thick soles that would "last a long time." They did. They were indestructible. It wouldn't surprise me if someone was still wearing them right now. Armor designed for the battlefield is probably less rugged than those shoes. So, that was the beginning of my fashion sorrows.

Even as a child, I understood the economy of those times, and why it was decided that my dresses should also be sturdy and long wearing. Plaid was chosen for me; light brown plaid and dark brown plaid, light gray plaid and dark gray plaid. The many bright colors in the plaid universe, the blues and reds, the happy pinks and greens were dismissed, even though they cost the same, as "not being practical." It was a dismal business. These dreary outfits were the most uninspiring clothes I would ever wear. I did not mind that they were homemade. The second I learned to sew, I made almost all my own clothes. But they did seriously lack joy.

Sure enough, amid the great trepidation of my very first day in a brand new place, I walked through the door of my first grade classroom into a sea of color. Girls were dressed in heavenly shades, some with matching ribbons in their perfectly curled hair. Worse though, were those darling shoes, the adorable and dainty Mary Jane's with the cute straps that some of them were wearing. I looked down at myself. In a room full of vibrant and animated parakeets, I was a frumpy, brown, uninteresting sparrow with ugly shoes. It was just a disaster. Added to the disadvantage of not knowing anyone and obviously not being "from there," the year became a grim exercise in endurance. It lasted from September until the end of May, and I counted the days, glad when it was mercifully over, and I could move somewhere else.

I got over being six, but I never got over those clothes. They still haunted me at age fifteen, as if insecurity was woven into every fiber and a battle continually waged to see who would prevail. I had discovered something important though, in about ten short seconds in that first grade classroom. There was a surprising power in clothes. They could make me feel worse or they could make me feel better. In some cases they could make me feel excessively better. It was a lesson I never forgot. If it was at all possible, I never again wanted to be standing anywhere in a frumpy brown dress and ugly shoes.

Insecurity, often the primary nemesis of adolescence, generously included me among its victims. There was ample evidence of that in my emotional aversion to plaid, saddle oxfords and the color brown. This was my own private battleground, the much contested territory of what to wear. Thankfully there was a new plaid in town, the popular madras plaid we were all destined to wear during our high school days. It came came in dozens of brilliant colors like hot pink, emerald green and lemon yellow. Someone far away had evidently seen the long trail of brown plaid damage and sent over to us an inspiring and liberating antidote. Just wearing it went a very long way in helping me down my road to emotional recovery.

*"This was my own private battleground, the much contested territory of what to wear."*

The newest beginning, my first day at Gulfport High School, finally came. I looked at my outfit in the mirror hoping it would be perfect. It wasn't bad. I chose a pretty, pale green A-line skirt and a pin-stripped Oxford blouse. The shoes, thank goodness, were pointy-toed flats, exactly what many of the other girls wore, and my perfectly curled hair was sprayed within an inch of its life. I was ready. I had reasons now, a good many, to believe I could do more than survive here. This was a perfect place, probably the most perfect place imaginable in which to think that.

The school year began in the tepid September days that still feel like summer and the winds off of the Gulf were still salty and warm. In the mornings I crowded into the building with the other students, walking the long halls of wood floors worn smooth by previous generations privileged to be part of the same world I now occupied. I began to make friends and be part of the usual conversations about the football game on Friday night, who had a date to the dance, who had just "broken up", and who was "back together." These vital questions were often as important and as life-changing as math or English would ever be.

I did finally start dating. I had the experiences now that my younger self dreamed of in my golden California days. My boyfriend always picked me up in his vintage car. We drove downtown, just the two of us with me on the front seat beside him and went to a movie, or we had hamburgers and milkshakes sitting in the car at a local drive-in. He took me to the big Friday night football games, the dances afterward in the gym and to Prom, unequivocally the social event of the year. Life around me began to settle in and resemble the lives of people who had always lived here. I started to feel a sensation new to me, something that I would call "normal."

Vintage and not-so-vintage cars, some with impressive engines, lined the streets around our school, driven by boys who understood the importance of impressive engines. This was frequently demonstrated at stop lights downtown after a movie on Saturday nights. These were short races with maximum acceleration, usually accompanied by some incendiary verbal exchange yelled out from car windows and clearly impossible to walk away from. I forgot to breathe a few times during these explosive episodes in my boyfriend's car, and I thought my heart might stop, but it never did.

The beach road was one long, constant parade of the best cars ever made. A black and white Ford, blue Buick or turquoise green Chevrolet with pristine upholstery took us a million miles up and down Highway 90 with the windows down, while we listened to songs like "I Want to Hold Your Hand," "Wooly Bully" or "Satisfaction." Songs by Johnny Rivers, the Beach Boys, Roy

Orbison, the Righteous Brothers and more played constantly on our car radios. I remember thinking that this was our music, and we would never, ever forget it. Years from now I would remember some song and where I was when I heard it. I would see faint, familiar faces and feel the same warm breeze stirring the night air.

We danced to those songs in the gym with our friends or at the Yacht Club to the music of our local band, the Weejuns or in the ballroom of some local hotel. Our music drifted in the light of a pale moon pouring through long, glass windows wide open to the night or underneath the ornate high ceilings of a ballroom, insulated from

the late chill of November. In the dim light of a patio party, couples held each other close, easing into quiet, slow songs under a canopy of dark oaks and palm trees. These were the hours we would remember; soft, familiar sounds floating out into the darkness of the Gulf, laughter and small talk while the night slowly slipped away toward an untroubled end.

———— ❧ ————

My friends and I had been raised as children in the 1950's, those days of un-air-conditioned homes and cars. It was a simpler time when we played hopscotch, marbles, jacks and ran around the yard at night catching lightning bugs in jars. Our neighborhood friends played baseball in someone's front yard, and we rode bikes until dark when we all had to go home to supper. We wore our skate keys on a string around our necks and roller skated up and down neighborhood sidewalks. The local drug store was our favorite place to go for ice cream or a Coke, and the familiar glass windows displayed books and gifts, a glimpse of candy bars in the case at the cash register inside and posters announcing a pancake breakfast on Saturday.

In Gulfport, one unofficial hub of life occupied a corner of 14th Street downtown, Triplett-Day Drug store with its facade of wide, faded green and white stripes. Everyone I knew came through its double glass doors. I became entangled with the flow of life here. Sitting at the lunch counter, I fell under the spell of this place, as if I had been here for a long, long time. I spent one whole afternoon talking with two of my friends about a much coveted, pink, semi-formal dress we saw in a shop window. We

strategized over handbags, debated having the shoes dyed to match and what jewelry would look the best. It was so thoroughly normal, so conventional. Whenever I left the drugstore I felt a little more normal and conventional myself.

Thousands of Gulfport High School students must have passed through those doors in all the long years Triplett-Day had been there. It was an indispensable institution then, as it had been for decades of other students with memories attached forever to that green-striped building on the corner downtown. Grown-ups came here, too. Businessmen sat here over coffee discussing the local economy or where redfish, drum or speckled trout had been or might be caught. They talked about the shipping out of the Port, what was the best route for the homecoming parade or plans for the annual Mississippi Deep Sea Fishing Rodeo held every July.

My friends and I bought our madras shirts, Weejun loafers, and long diaphanous prom dresses from the multitude of shoe stores, dress shops and clothing stores downtown. Our feet walked those sidewalks, and we stood on those corners watching Christmas and Homecoming parades. Our main street, 25th Avenue, ended at the intersection of Highway 90, with a view of the Gulf and a broad park wrapping the long edges of blue water. Jones Park was a sweeping, green expanse, Mississippi's "front yard," connecting the busy area around the Port of Gulfport. We had band and majorette practice there, marching up and down in the sandy grass, and we watched boats go out from the Small Craft Harbor and the Yacht Club. The boundaries of our small world essentially stretched from the streets and shops of downtown to the Gulf, the sidewalks full of shoppers, businessmen, fishermen and tourists coming and going against a background that was almost always perfectly blue.

The defining presence of the Gulf began at the park, reaching all the way across the wide, unending horizon. The Gulf was an absolute in a world that relied on it. High tide was sometimes a forceful reminder of its power. The waves in all their midnight blue intensity announced it, crashing in that monotonous rhythm that was so soothing. Later, as the tide went out, sandbars emerged slick and flat. They were covered with little villages of hopeful birds, attached to each other like tiny delegations on the fingers of sand as if this was all the land in the world. I always wondered, when the tide came in, where did the birds go? Did they have their own version of Triplett-Day somewhere, crowding into little bird-booths and talking to one another about the irritating propensities of the sea and the annoyance of constantly rearranging themselves? The birds might be displaced regularly but like their predecessors, they belonged here. Their little colonies would always occupy the

variable expanse of water and sand, shifting tenuously with the tides and the blue-gray ceiling high above them.

The Gulf had a thousand faces, and I never grew tired of looking at it. The sunsets were glowing things, ephemeral and radiant, and often the entire world was pink. I sat on the sea wall looking at it and thought, who could not possibly be moved by a world bathed in pink? But even more moving, more spectacular, if that's possible, was the full moon of warm summer shining down on the bare waves of the Gulf, its highway of light intense against the night. It was certainly romantic seen from anywhere, and it drew me to itself so completely that I was perfectly contented to just sit there and bask indefinitely in its light. That moon, shining down on Mississippi, shining down on the Gulf, became a permanent part of my mental history. I enjoyed being wrapped in its light in the same intoxicating way I enjoyed being smothered in Southern greenery. There were a

great many comforts here, living in the light of a perpetual cocoon. If happiness could be coaxed from finite moments in time like this, if by some miracle, there was a convergence of forces that left a lasting goodness behind them, then I had surely been the recipient of that.

The Gulf Coast as I eventually understood it, unfolded steadily as an expanse securely wedged in time, attached by snug moorings set in place long ago. It had a specific sense of constancy, a past and a present entirely filling the edges of the Gulf with a litany of family histories. The men and women I met here, and my friends, were a continuing reflection of that past. I simply never met any better people anywhere. Mostly they were born and raised in Gulfport and knew each other since kindergarten, but they were unfailingly kind to strangers. Here was a world of charming civility entirely self-contained, a kind of Camelot resting invisibly everywhere in tranquil, halcyon days of salt air and moonlight shining on the Gulf. I still see my friends, those so-pretty girls and good-looking boys, waving from a Homecoming float or performing in a talent show, or wearing letter jackets and smiling through a car window at the unequaled world around us.

The power of this place claimed me, asserting a kind of divine ownership over my soul, unfolding in that slow way a gardenia has before its scent permeates the air. A reminder of that power was in every apricot sunset or luminous sunrise, or the movement of every wave against the long, serpentine stretches of sand. I felt changed now, adopted by this pleasing world, with others like me, who came from so far away to find it. There was a tranquility here, a natural progression, a predominant cadence to everything. My own deep desire from the beginning was simply to find my place in it. In the end, I both lost myself and found myself, or a more complete version of myself, and that was enough for me, more than enough.

*Chapter 6*

# THE SAVIOR

inter descended on Gulfport December 31, 1963, New Year's Eve. Snow fell in an avalanche of soft, fluffy, white flakes, and the drifts were deep for a coastal town in the South. That never happened. It seldom even tried to snow here, but it had succeeded as a last parting gift to the year, and the world

outside was cold and crisp and white. It was a bad beginning, and inside I sat at a window waiting for God.

I was completely absorbed in the comfortable atmosphere of the coast. This was starting to feel like home, and I was so familiar now with the everyday activities of high school life that my feelings of being newly transplanted had almost completely gone away. Settled in among warm classmates and friends, the chilly winter days didn't seem cold at all, and as the year advanced, so did my confidence. But then, in the midst of all this newly acquired confidence, I did something rash. I committed a blunder so bad that it went well past the point of no return. I was beyond salvation.

This uncharacteristic lapse in judgment came one day at school in a small, innocent conversation that grew legs of its own and raced ahead of me like wildfires in high winds. As we came down from our high school's second floor, packed like sardines on the wide, creaky stairs, someone casually said how fun it would be to have a New Year's Eve party. I think I said something very vague in agreement. By the end of the day and a few exchanges later, without quite thinking it through, I had invited more than a few friends and some almost complete strangers to a New Year's Eve party at my house. They all said they would come. I struggled to figure out exactly how this happened, and immediately I started to feel it, the crushing terror from two different worlds; part of me afraid they wouldn't come and part of me afraid that they would.

81

I tried vainly in the days ahead to think of a way out, but every time I attempted to cancel the whole thing, some person came up to me and said how excited they were to come. I was woefully inept at having a social event, and I was equally unskilled at canceling one. I remembered a few things from other parties I had been to. I knew we needed refreshments and some kind of music. I thought maybe I could make cookies, punch and some kind of dip to have with chips. Punch was the only beverage I had ever seen at parties, so I felt fairly safe with that. I decided we could play records on the stereo in the living room and maybe people would dance. It was all a hopeful fantasy. I could see that later.

In spite of every effort I made to simply will it away, the end of December came. The days evaporated one by one, ticking down slowly and inevitably, completely eviscerating Christmas. It came and went uncelebrated in my mind. All I could think about was the one stark day looming ahead. I thought about prisoners in a courtroom awaiting their sentence, waiting for judgment to fall, harsh and swift. There would be no reprieve, not for them, the imaginary miscreants in my mind, and not for me.

Tuesday, New Year's Eve, came finally, inevitably and brought with it more than a foot of snow, according to WLOX. The landscape outside was completely white and silent as if the whole world had suddenly stopped breathing. I looked out at it and a small hopeful thought appeared in my desperate little mind. Maybe the roads were simply impassable, and no one could travel. No one could actually get here to my unreachable little party. They would all give their apologies later about how their parents wouldn't let them come.

I would give them an appreciative smile like it was completely understandable, and that would be that. That could work. Definitely. Or maybe, they would all arrive in a holiday mood, and the evening would be a smashing success. That could work, too.

I harbored these conflicting thoughts all day long while we baked cookies and made punch. I didn't even tell my parents about the festive gathering to be held under their roof until a couple of days before when there was no point of remaining in denial. All that snowy day, as the afternoon slipped away we baked, decorated, shoveled snow and prepared as soldiers do for battle. My Latin class had acquainted me with gladiators adorning the annals of Roman history. They came back now to haunt me. That quote, "…those who are about to die salute you," seemed appropriate in ways I could not have imagined before.

I put on a red party dress, the disguise of a confident hostess and stood at my bedroom window looking out at the fallen snow, bargaining with God. I prayed for the evening's success. I think I promised Him the usual things, that I would be eternally good, and I would never ask Him for anything ever again. I may have even promised to be a missionary. I was desperate. I didn't take these prayers lightly because I felt He knew about my troubles and had always known about them. I harbored a small hope that people full of holiday joy would actually come, and I tried to imagine cars of expectant party-goers pulling up in front of my house.

They did. They came, in spite of the ominous streets, to our small house in our small neighborhood, driven there by doubtful parents unwilling to allow their teenagers to be "out on the roads on a night like this." More people came than I had even invited, people I didn't even know. Their expectations of an evening of unbridled and hopefully unchaperoned revelry brought them all to my door, and now I felt the formidable weight of social responsibility. It was my duty to entertain these disappointed revelers for four long hours. Exhilaration and hope, punctuated by moments of terror, preceded their arrival. Terror would be all that was left. Exhilaration evaporated in the first thirty minutes. Hope, soon after. I was forced to preside over the melancholy demise of this failed social experiment until midnight came, an eternity away.

The air was heavy inside. There were too many people in a too-small house, and we all wound up sitting in an uneasy circle around the living room. The stereo played, but no one danced. My parents turned off a couple of bright lamps, hoping to add a note of dim ambiance and then retreated to the kitchen. The party food, carefully arranged on the dining room table, provided a tiny source of diversion while we wandered in small circles around it making feeble attempts at small talk, but it was clear that fun was not on the menu. Definitely not. The evening was one long slow train wreck.

I had plenty of time to think, but everything seemed to be happening in slow motion, like I was watching it all from a distance. I thought once maybe I was dead. Having ascended, I could look down now with pity on the abject misery below. But, no. I breathed slowly a couple of times. I was alive. I only wished I was dead. I thought then of my father's plan to let me finish high school here. Suddenly, moving somewhere else seemed like a really good idea. I would talk to him about it. At some new school in my future, no one would know about this horrible night, and I could pretend it never happened. I was already mentally packing my bags when something truly extraordinary happened.

At an obscure moment in the unfolding gloom, when the evening seemed irretrievably lost in a dark abyss, a tiny ray of light arrived. It appeared in the form of a person: Mack, "the savior." Mack was a senior, very good looking, very cool, and somehow in my very first days at Gulfport High School, for reasons that were never clear to me, we became friends. He took me to dances sometimes, and I hung out with him and some of his friends. He always seemed to appear when I needed him, and now he appeared again, miraculously unscathed by the tenacious grip of the icy, snow-covered streets. I was unprepared when I saw his car pull up and park in front of the house. Pulling his guitar case from the car, he came up the walk, smiling in his nonchalant way and then walked through our front door into the church-like atmosphere.

Mack's most enviable gift was that casual way he had of seeming completely comfortable in any situation. He always just had an extraordinary degree of charm. He radiated good will with amazing ease, and tonight his presence had an astonishing effect. He was my good friend. He was here to save what could be salvaged from the evening, and his low chuckles of amusement as he settled into playing a song familiar to us all, "Puff the Magic Dragon," made the immediate future substantially brighter. The mood lightened. People chatted. They listened to Mack play, and our little moment improved enough that we all stopped praying for midnight to come soon. We sang "Old Lang Syne." Everyone breathed a sigh of relief, and then the parents came.

Mack, in no particular hurry, left last of all, strolling back to his car as if nothing terribly unusual had happened. But he left me with a debt I would owe him forever. He had truly saved me from a fate worst than death, and I understood then why people were tempted to fall down in worship at the feet of angels who were bearers of deliverance and good news. In the days and months that followed, I thanked him every now and then for being there that night. He always half-shrugged in that usual way of his, as if saving inept and unsophisticated girls from disaster was something he routinely did before breakfast. That snowy night I learned quite a few things, but one stood out: when the "savior" shows up, he might be in a black '59 Ford and carrying a guitar case.

I never forgot that. And it seemed like, maybe, people brought little bits of salvation to each other all the time in ways wholly unexpected and unexplained. Other friends in our class were a litany of goodness without even being aware of it. One friend danced ballet, like me. She was new too, even newer than I was. She sparkled. Her joy was contagious and we found a kinship in being "the new people." Both of us were transient souls. Our expectations of forming lasting friendships were limited, so finding each other such good company was like having an extra present to open on Christmas.

In the Gulfport High School Band I found some of the same unexpected friendships. My own skill level playing the bass clarinet was pretty basic, but we had some excellent musicians, and we performed really well at the state marching band competitions.

*"... it seemed like, maybe, people brought little bits of salvation to each other all the time in ways wholly unexpected and unexplained."*

The band was like a family of sorts, probably because of all the hours we spent practicing together and traveling on road trips to the football games. Marching up and down in Jones Park occupied a major part of our lives, working on the routines and music for the half-time shows. Those of us who were majorettes went to Hattiesburg for summer majorette camp. Our small group of girls, so pretty and fun to be with, performed in the parades downtown and in the half-time shows, and we spent hours together after school at majorette practice. I can't think of any other company in which I would have been happier, and I still love the memory of all those hours we spent together twirling our batons.

It seemed to me that almost every classmate I knew well had some specific quality that defined them and would remind me of them always. More than a few were brilliant thinkers and scholars. Some were professional enthusiasts. We had exceptional beauties, fabulous singers, musicians, tennis players, golfers and ball players. The bar of excellence at Gulfport High School was set pretty high. That atmosphere created some lasting effects. The pursuit of

UNIVERSITY OF SOUTHERN MISSISSIPPI

excellence, the concept of happiness and what those things looked like in real life, were things I was just beginning to think about.

A counselor at school, a lady with whom I spent many "saving" hours was a seamless figure among the others. She was a sounding board for my emerging thoughts. For me, the concept of happiness was an amorphous thing, perhaps a little like jello, impossible to really get your hands around, and it kept moving all the time. I looked up the definition of happiness once. It was a little vague. It said, "a feeling or showing pleasure or contentment." In a psychology book I found happiness mentioned as "subjective well being." Those were not very satisfying answers for someone like me. I was interested in what happiness actually looked like. For me, life was a sliding scale of sorts, with degrees of happiness at one end and degrees of unhappiness (sometimes known as misery) at the other. I wondered if the moments weren't just balanced against each other. At some point "happiness" simply outweighed "unhappiness" slightly, just enough to create a happy memory, a moment in time strong enough to overpower the currents that generally raged against it.

Happiness and the quest to find it wasn't the only thing this lady and I talked about. We talked about lots more; how to see the world through different eyes, as less of a visitor and more of a participant. I was dug in as a visitor. I had years of experience as one of life's visitors, and I was only beginning to understand the skills required to be a participant. She was an example of a successful person engaged in a larger world, and for the first time I saw what it might be like to have a vision of something bigger than myself. The young age of fifteen had crept up on me, leaving one foot somewhere in my old childhood and the other in a world I didn't recognize. The biggest part of me wanted this world I did not yet know to be warm and welcoming. I wanted a place with some safety in it and some silent spaces that I could fill with my own thoughts, instead of borrowed ones.

Eventually, in uncontrived moments, I got small hints of what my own thoughts might actually be. I sensed a hesitant contentment and the first signs of courage. My best thoughts came in the stillness looking out at the Gulf, rare moments that lacked the fingerprints of others on them and around them, holding them until they lost the breath of life and became artificial, and venerated. Some moments stood still on their own without support or effort, existing like stars in a dark universe, fading and reappearing an eternity away. And sometimes, the moments were here like a faithful guide when I was unsure of the way. A casual observer beside me looking out at the same blue horizon might see only a Gulf in fading light. A keen observer might see more, a vastness that suggested images of the past. But when I looked at the Gulf, I saw it as more of a sanctuary with all kinds of things in it, little bits of eternity and maybe even little bits of happiness.

It was easy sometimes to feel a little like an unstudied mystic. Time always waited for me here, but I might have felt it with the gratitude of the young who only recognize the proper worth of a thing long after it's gone. I sat looking out at the Gulf until the relentless, purple shadows finally deepened like the pages of a book slowly turning toward an inexorable end that can't be ignored. I always wanted to stay here in these last smoldering fires of light, only turning away finally into the night, with the wind behind me.

I had hundreds of Gulf sunsets stored in my memory and the emotions that go with them. And I had hundreds more images of high school friends who were there too, looking out at the same sunsets and thinking how extraordinary they were. For some reason, descending dusk had an inspiring effect. We had conversations then

that I don't remember ever happening anywhere else. We sat in cars parked out by the pier facing the beach with the windows down and salt air blowing through, or we walked down and sat with our toes in the sand close to the small waves rolling up on the beach. My friends and I were extravagant in those days in regard to our futures. I had illusions of myself living in Italy. Don't ask me why. But, the idea of Europe seemed irresistibly romantic and an intriguing picture of sophisticated independence. One friend was captivated by New York and possibly life on the stage. Others just wanted to be away, to experience the exhilaration of someplace new.

Most of us, at one time or another, spent week-ends or had longer visits on some college campus, and we were already experiencing that exhilaration we were looking for, the thrill of someplace new.

I liked the freedom of it, the feeling of the dorms, the excitement of parties in fraternity or sorority houses. It was an overpowering experience. Walking across the campus at the University of Southern Mississippi was the first time I ever remember feeling grown up. There was alcohol everywhere, too, and the effect it had on people was very interesting and entertaining. I realized how limited my little world had been.

Campus parties were usually full of bodies crushed together into dark rooms where live bands played the songs we loved, and we danced on small, tight dance floors until way into the night. Everybody had the same idea: having an excessively good time. I could see that college was going to be something I liked very much, although studying might seriously interfere with my social life. My friends and I came back home from these little excursions into college life swept away by the prospect of a tantalizing future, one without too many rules and an extreme amount of freedom.

*" I realized on a regular basis, how helpful it was to have friends, especially good friends"*

I went up to college football games, sometimes on weekends, when friends invited me. They knew I would find the campus wonderfully exciting. I did find it exciting. I usually arrived enthusiastically with my overnight bag and stayed with a friend in her dorm. I felt like an actual college girl, sharing her room in the absence of her roommate. I borrowed some college-girl clothes from her, and we spent a huge amount of time getting ready for the football game. The enthusiasm associated with college football was new to me. Sitting in the stands with all the other cheering students gave me another heady feeling of being grown up. I could see myself belonging here or somewhere like it, going to classes, sitting in the student union and walking across campus with an armload of books.

I realized on a regular basis, how helpful it was to have friends, especially good friends like the essential figures in my Gulfport High School world. I was unfamiliar with real, lasting relationships until I came here. I just didn't know what they looked like. It took me a while to realize that friends here were a source of unconditional dependability, for each other and for me. We just typically didn't let each other down. The usual adolescent adversity lurked around every corner. We had our share of bad days, bad test grades and bad experiences. We lost games, lost competitions, lost boyfriends, lost girlfriends and occasionally, in some overwhelming moments, we lost ourselves. But someone always showed up with encouragement and a helping hand. We called and someone came. This was practice for the years ahead when we encountered real adversity. We would be dependable friends. Someone would call and we would come. It took me a while to see it. But slowly, I saw something important. Among the lavish gifts we all gave each other, among the generosity and kindness and encouragement, I recognized the beginnings, the first triumphant hints of what I might describe as happiness.

*Chapter 7*

# THE LADIES

I had a quiet affair, a romance of subtle intensity that dominated a slender sequence of sublime days. I remember the beginning, the first days when I counted the minutes until I could be here again, comfortable against the worn chintz cushions. I wondered if anyone knew, if they suspected that I came here and stayed for hours. My friends had their own interests; parties, cars, sailing and sometimes decadent

liquid temptations, all benign amusements of the sunbaked world outside. But indistinct forces drew me here, and they were simply too powerful to resist. Those stolen hours would dominate my thoughts, the unfading memory of them surviving for decades. When I think of those insular days now, they seem like a parallel universe that I still live in, both here and there at the same time. That must be true because we cannot "un-live" where we have been. I couldn't imagine ever leaving behind the unabbreviated devotion I felt here, and standing in the doorway one afternoon I admitted it to myself finally. It was too late to go back now. I wanted to stay here and live forever in this perfect place.

I had fallen deeply, passionately in love with ardent figures who promised to never leave me, and I believed them completely. They were mythical characters, sophisticated and unburdened by mortality. They lived far beyond constricting limitations of everyday life, traveling through time, not in automobiles or passenger trains, but in bound and printed pages. I had not been seduced by anything remotely made of flesh and blood, but by literature, the worn interiors of books stacked high around me. The ancient volumes seemed to recognize me, inviting me in like one of their own. The timeless pages I loved were the literary sediment of the ages written by the

immortals of the past. I should have seen it coming after that feeling, the rush of excitement carrying my first Dick and Jane beginner reader home from school. I read the words, sounding them out slowly until they became sentences, and then they became stories with places and characters who said and did interesting things. It was an explosive beginning.

My soul longed for more. I desperately wanted, needed more books, whole rooms of them rising from floor to ceiling like literary wall paper. I was inexorably drawn toward anything with a cover and pages inside. The genres of the written word were unknown to me then. If left to myself, I just picked up anything that might be lying around and read it. As it turned out, I was left to myself quite a bit, enough for me to further my literary education in an extremely original and highly entertaining way.

In the dark basement of my grandparents' house, in endless sprawling stacks, was enough reading material to last anyone a lifetime. So, when I was nine years old, I spent an entire summer working my way undisturbed through years of true crime magazines. They were fascinating. The covers usually had pictures of steel-jawed, handsome men, some sort of gun, and voluptuous women in various states of alarm. Inside were highly-detailed stories of extortion, robberies and murders or attempted murders. The detective was usually a dubious fellow with shady connections, and after a while I could tell in a few pages which way the story would go. Then, I could just skip to the good part. The provocative and grateful victim, now completely smitten by the impressive skills of her hero, sat having drinks with him in the smoky darkness of some bar, planning the escape from their urban nightmare. Usually they planned to go to some exotic place like Morocco or Buenos Aires where they could live without being found and killed, again. This was endlessly entertaining and the writing was actually very good. As I think about it now, it was comparable to a college level course in Crime Fiction, only with a lot more material to cover.

In mere months that summer I became a crime expert, in addition to increasing my reading comprehension level and acquiring a colorful and extensive new vocabulary. I sometimes took my milk and cookies down there, an incongruous contrast to the cigarettes and Bourbon usually associated with such scintillating material. No one ever looked for me in those cluttered regions below the stairs. If anyone inquired about Linda someone would say, "Oh, she's just down in the basement." They never asked what I was doing down there. I guess they figured it's just a basement, how much trouble can she get into. Not a lot, and I did get quite an education, one that would attract me later to Agatha Christie and her intrepid protagonist Hercule Poirot. At that young age I should have been reading Francis Hodgson Burnett. Years later I did happily find her story, *The Secret Garden*. It had an appealing charm, except for the disappointing absence of lethal weapons and terrifying escapes hidden among contraband in the cargo hold of some tramp steamer bound for Cartagena. Maybe I was just expecting too much now.

At seventeen, the age of wrenchingly powerful emotions, I found myself in the most fortunate circumstances imaginable. I became a perennial guest in a white house, the one that contained the room of my dreams. I sat there on the floor among the stacks, the books piled everywhere, lining the walls of faded floral paper and pale decorous woodwork up to the high ceiling of the glorious library. At the narrower end of the room there was one long window for light with a view of the garden. I came to be here accidentally and in the way such things are often arranged, unexpectedly. That morning, the beginning of it all, was warm with the heavy humid air of summer, sticky in the way that made a cotton shirt cling to damp skin. Even the slightest breeze did not pass unnoticed.

I walked along our street, Venetian Gardens, that led up from the beach, and I stopped inside a picket gate to help recapture an enormous stack of library books being unsuccessfully managed by a semi-matronly woman. She was removing them from one of those old station wagons with sides made of wooden panels. A few steps, mere moments later still juggling the books, I was standing in the semidarkness of a vintage world while the lady identified herself. Our small conversation and my hesitant interest in the stacks of books gave me immediate admission to their library and later, to

the lives of the two venerable ladies who lived there. Why they invited me into the quiet rhythms of their home was a mystery to me, but that very first morning they did. They may have seen a lostness in me and warmed to the idea of an opportunity to exercise their innate Christian charity.

I still see it, all of it, in my mind: my feet in white tennis shoes standing there on the irregular grass of our familiar street, my hand on the gate of the white picket fence ready to lightly swing it open and the air heavy with the scent of salt air and magnolias. The approach was always the same as it probably had been for decades: the uneven path of disappearing brick through the slightly ragged front yard heavy with the shade of ancient live oaks, their spreading limbs of weeping moss reaching far across the lawn.

The landscape was grand in a small sort of way, only because of the startling size of the vegetation that dominated the expanse of ground stretching with tenacious fingers toward the Gulf. Azaleas and camellias grew like wild things, their branches twisting into extravagant leafy walls. Cast iron plant, firmly rooted in large circular clumps beneath each massive tree was a favorite of mine mainly because it was so reliably green, resilient and dependable. I would later look for those qualities in people. The sprawling lawn itself, gripped in a constant battle against the elements of sea and drifting sand, had the appearance of a battle-scarred warrior who was somewhat diminished but still ready to fight another day. It struggled mightily, and in some places succeeded, becoming rewardingly lush and green. It co-existed in a

101

kind of détente with thick borders of liriope that stretched in long beds around the house and into the garden behind, its picket fence a deteriorating home for the moss and lichens that clung to it here and there like little pieces of history. The oleanders lived there, thick with pink and coral blooms. They stood as tall as the house and were as impenetrable as bamboo, forming fortress-like, medieval castle walls. They were the silent guardians of this luxuriant world, standing resolute there for ages upon ages, framing the edges of the lawn with the white house and its front porch that looked toward the sea.

The house set back at an angle not quite facing the Gulf. Like the other houses closer to the water on our street, it was built to capture the sea breezes and views of blue waves. It stood comfortably behind its picket fence on our long, shaded lane in Mississippi City, a small community securely occupying its own space on the white sand that stretched like a glittering ribbon between Gulfport and Biloxi. The homes that actually faced the Gulf were larger, grander than the others, the houses further from the water becoming examples of receding greatness. Sitting as it did, the less pretentious home of the ladies was a pleasant balance between the imposing status of her larger sisters and the casual charm of a raised cottage. The sloping roof, weathered gray, and resident birds of exactly the same color were the first signs of its friendliness followed by the front porch with its high, blue ceiling and aging wicker furniture. Faded green shutters in perpetual need of paint lined long windows entirely covered on one side by possessive vegetation. A flight of narrow and slowly deteriorating brick steps clung to the gray planks of the porch, and beyond them, a heavy white front door opened to a slightly irregular entry. Inside in the semidarkness, the pale glow of obviously antique lamps lit a vintage world of patterned carpets, somber furniture and more stacks of books.

A long wall with windows beyond opened to a meandering hallway that led toward the kitchen and library which sat opposite each other. They were joined by a small, pleasant nook with a narrow bench upholstered in a needlepoint of a once brilliant, but now pale iris. The kitchen itself, which I never entered but only glimpsed from its small doorway, had cabinets of pale turquoise, faded now, but still determined to make an effort at cheerfulness.

*"I wanted to be in the space sitting among the chintz cushions, as if I had always been there, belonged there and had perhaps accumulated a little dust myself."*

Not a large room, the library still had an imposing quality about it with shelves and shelves of books wrapping the room on three sides. All jammed together happily in their slightly dusty world, the volumes rested there on the shelves as they had for decades. When I came here I always reached for them carefully, as if by disturbing the dust I might also disturb some venerable author's musings or interfere with his repose, something I was loathe to do. I wanted to be in the space sitting among the chintz cushions, as if I had always been there, belonged there and had perhaps accumulated a little dust myself.

Here I could take my time and appreciate the dated colors usual in old books; faded green, brown, blue, black and occasionally red or pink. It was as if, simply by being old, they were now more mysterious, more inviting. None of the shiny, impossibly bright, modern book covers were allowed to interfere with this happy arrangement, intruding as interlopers upon the pleasant characters who had all been here together for so long.

My experiences in the library were very similar to visiting the grave of someone now gone from me, remembering our times together. The words, the last words of some person were contained in all these pages now grown brown around the edges. They sat here on shelves waiting for someone to read them, to understand them. I wondered if somewhere above, authors sat together looking down, waiting for someone like me to turn through the pages of their books and find the thing they had written that would be the salvation of her soul. Would these departed authors know? Would they say to one another, "Oh look. She's found it." And would they all nod and smile at one another, glad that their words still lived on? I thought invisible conversations like that happened here, if I listened for them.

My cloister was filled silently and completely with the relics of another age as companions and immersed in the comforting feel and smell of old books and old worlds. One of the ladies who lent me this space would come sometimes to suggest certain passages and authors to me: Ruskin, Kipling, Welty or others worthy of my attention. Then they left me there blessedly alone to ruminate, cocooned among the books until I was ready to emerge.

Every time I came to this house, I felt its power to stir me. That is what I remember most, a singularly untroubled recollection; the shadowed rooms beneath high ceilings, lace-paneled windows, the musty smell of age, old rugs, old wallpaper and old books in advancing disarray on antique tables. Heavy shades created an almost gloomy effect, but more what I would call serious. These were serious rooms for serious people, and they had a transporting effect which was, in its own way, really spectacular. This place had a strange compelling quality about it, and I simply melted away here, surgically absorbed into a happy oblivion. Time, disappointment, apprehensions simply disappeared inside the walls of that house.

It was easy, very easy to be drawn into the lives and books of the ladies and their pleasant ways. Their house was a charmingly sedate world marked by unalterable behavior, and I thought of it as a kind of sanctuary. The ladies didn't demand things. They requested them. They did everything with genteel self-restraint. They were like that. I never suffered the threat of being engulfed by their personalities. My benefactors did not thrust themselves upon me or upon each other, with a constant and draining torrent of words or conversations about the weather or the state of their health. They just left me blessedly alone.

I heard their voices sometimes, almost inaudible, in other rooms. But the silence was the real force in that house, affecting me deeply as if it were stronger, more powerful than even the words themselves. Every time I went there and the front door closed safely behind me, I was redeemed by a dependable quiet. Only a respectable clock ticked faintly while the delicious silence descended until I was completely immersed in it. Fluent in soundlessness, it spoke without conventional means and extended far beyond illusionary boundaries. The silence was just itself, and when I was there, I could be myself, too.

I went there as often as I could, escaping into the company of the two somewhat ancient owners. The one I met first, slightly less-aged than the other, often appeared in gabardine slacks the color of caramel like those one might see on safari, and a loose faded shirt that made her appear somehow exotic and sensible all at the same time. She had pleasant, even features and her hair, shoulder-length and graying, hung loose and un-styled. These were all indications of a woman decidedly un-fussy, unpretentious and very much at home with herself. In time I came to see that she was all of those things.

The older one of the two wore the shapeless, dark print dresses and sensible, low heeled, lace-up shoes of another era. Her hair was pulled back in a twisted bun, and there was no sign that makeup of any kind had ever been applied to either of their calm, unlined faces. I had no idea of the economics of the household. They did not seem to be poor, but simply choosing to live in a comfortable frugality. Their entire environment appeared comfortably frozen in time, maybe 1940, as if they had then all they needed and simply did not buy another dress or shoes or stick of furniture after that. They seemed to be living daily in a kind of period movie set almost as actors, moving methodically about in the clothes and habits of aged women, masters of slow deliberate movement and temperate speech. I seriously doubted if they had ever been animated, and conversation moved as everything else, in slow motion.

A few times I lent a hand to the younger of them when she capably brought in groceries or stacks of library books from the equally aged car. It always struck me as odd though, out of character somehow for them to ever go "out" and bring things "in." Their world felt so complete and self-contained. I found this retiring atmosphere so pleasing and at odds with the currents of my family life swirling beyond its walls. I missed the temperate quiet when I wasn't there.

The ladies and I did have casual conversations, light exchanges when I had been invited to join them on the deep wine-colored sofas in their sitting room. They asked if I had seen some of the historical sights on the coast like Fort Massachusetts on Ship Island, or knew about the renowned Ring in the Oak. Years ago they had seen it and the Friendship Oak farther down the coast. They remembered the Father Ryan House with a large tree, a palm, growing right out of the front steps. Nature interested them, and they were especially fond of trees and birds. Apparently, in some decade of their lives on the coast, they had been exposed to pelicans, ospreys and blue herons. They pointed those out to me sometimes in the illustrated volumes on the shelves. I think they might have begun to feel a slight responsibility for my education and added little bits here and there that they considered useful. It seemed important and entirely appropriate that I reflected well on them now that I was identified with their household.

The particular stillness of their quiet, pleasant library gave me time to read and think about what my life might be, or could be. The ladies usually let me meander through the hall and find my own way to the library now. I was at home among the pink peonies and roses of the fading wallpaper, and they left me to muse for long un-interrogated hours about classes at school or fragmentary plans for the future. Conventional paths to stellar success seemed a little overwhelming, and there was something about the safety of mediocrity that appealed to me. They didn't judge me for this. I think they hoped that here among their books, I would find my own good path forward. Then, they could breath a small sigh of relief that their almost daily contributions to my personal advancement had been rewarded.

From the very beginning, the dim library of vintage books was easily the most irresistible of all the rooms in the house. In fact, it seemed like all paths led to it. The other rooms were introductory, welcoming and functional but at some point everyone ended up here, drawn to the faded grandeur of the book-lined walls. The affection of the ladies for the imperfect volumes was obvious to me from the very beginning, from the very first minute they led me to this room and I stepped inside. I suspected they spent their own hours here, gently running their aged fingers over the worn book covers, remembering their favorite lines and communing with the dead as I had.

I was part of their world now, joined with them in a congenial history contained within the literary boundaries of this room. There were little bits of solace here, maybe even little bits of heaven, the kind found in old things and old places. Profound moments were here too, liberated in a room of faded floral wallpaper, at a window overlooking a garden, in the quiet company of the best words and the best people who left them for us to help us find our way.

## CHAPTER 8

# A GREEN WORLD

MY FATHER

My father was a sometime businessman and sometime golf pro who loved the game more than life itself, and I had been practically living in pro shops ever since I could remember. Golf courses everywhere became home to me, with long fairways and greens for rooms and white carpets of curving sand traps. This could account for my early infatuation with Southern vegetation, and why I imagined there were stories everywhere in dripping moss and landscapes bathed in perfect light. From the beginning, a trail through these green fantasies had been forged for me, luckily by someone who knew how. I merely followed him dutifully into a verdant world that was a kind of shelter for me and always would be.

It was a pretty world, and I loved the game and this leafy realm almost as much as he did. In Gulfport, living in our perfect Mississippi paradise, my father played at the Broadwater Sea Course. It sat on the Gulf along Highway 90, framed by water, white sand and shifting blue-gray sky. Venetian Gardens, our street, was a narrow lane tucked behind the tall pines bordering the course. We lived in a house among the long row of others stretching back from the

WAITING FOR MY FATHER

Gulf. The venerable ladies who lent me their library lived here too, farther down our street toward the beach.

When I was not at school or in my own personal neighborhood library, I was often here in my usual province, bathed in the greenery, waiting for my father to begin or finish the front or back nine. I spent years on courses from Mississippi to California waiting for him this way or walking along with him while he played or sometimes driving the cart, my very favorite thing. Usually studied and quiet, he came to life here, effortlessly mastering the connection between the irons and woods, and their application in his current assault on bunkers, sand traps and ponds. They were all hazards to be duly noted and overcome with careful planning and execution. I loved watching him hit a long straight drive or perfect chip shot.

He was certainly more at ease and more himself here than anywhere else. I suspected that even when he wasn't on the golf course, he was thinking about being on it or engaged in planning to be on it. That he wanted me there, that he took me with him, had a great many benefits, and I tried to take advantage of every one of them. I was completely at home among the towering trees in these extravagant park-like settings, walking along with him for hours, almost more at home than in any real house.

My father and some of the other players who walked those long fairways together took on gentle personas of the past, the captivating past of the 1940's. They had lived in that decade, and they brought the conversations of those days along with them. It almost seemed sometimes that we were still living there, as though the great ones, Sam Snead, Ben Hogan, Byron Nelson and the dashing and colorful Walter Hagan were present among us. The men still told their stories, still talked of some impossible shot they had made. All the scenarios began much the same way, "Hey, remember that time on eighteen when he chipped it in for a birdie..." or some other similarly brilliant recount.

The recollections of these men, the manners associated with them and the environment they suggested drew me into a past I might have been made for. I wondered then and sometimes now if I had been born in the right decade. The images from Hollywood movies of that era captured my imagination; the automobiles, the clothes, glasses of lemonade on a shady front porch, the semi-antique charms of it all were irresistible. It was so real that some mornings when I first woke up, I didn't quite know where I was. The rose colored wallpaper and lace tie-back curtains of my imagination, the smell of bacon cooking downstairs and the sound of the milkman leaving glass bottles at the door were missing, as if I had somehow awakened in someone else's reality. Maybe that was another reason to love the house of the ladies because there I could actually almost be in another era.

The men like my father who had known the decade of the 1940's and the ones that preceded it, were the friendliest visitors in this unblemished green world. We shared the lush avenues stretching before us, absorbed by the most agreeable surroundings anywhere. The signature square-faced greens designed by Donald Ross were famous, and it was extremely important whether they were fast or slow. Among ourselves we used phrases and words like Bermuda and Tifgreen, Bentgrass and Zoysia, a vocabulary of place, an identifying language, as if this green environment was a remote country all to itself. Casual exchanges between the players used other standard words like handicap, birdie, double bogey, short iron, wedge and sometimes Frank Sinatra.

My father thought the big bands of the 1940's like Tommy Dorsey and Benny Goodman were the only real music, and he enjoyed singers like Bing Crosby and Frank Sinatra. His friends, these nice men, all agreed with him. I grew to love Frank. Who was I to disagree with these pleasant men, these authorities and music arbiters around me? Fragments of music, the great songs of a wartime era I heard from childhood, seemed to follow us everywhere. Their melodies could be faintly heard sometimes, whistled near the clubhouse by someone loading or unloading their clubs for the day. I loved the gentle, persuasive harmonies, the echoes of those slow, old songs like "I'll Be Seeing You" drifting lost among the pines.

In addition to my music education, I even learned to identify the evils lurking everywhere that were capable of inflicting great harm to the sanctified turf. My father taught me that turf was a holy thing, to be groomed, caressed, watered, mowed, coaxed and manicured continually into a thing of celestial beauty. Unforgivable transgressions like the failure to properly replace a divot were cause for expulsion from the sacred brotherhood. Some things can be forgiven in this life, but not that. It symbolized poor character. Banishment was swift, and in my memory, no one was ever re-admitted.

Demeanor mattered to my father and to everyone else I ever met on a golf course anywhere. It was a gentlemen's game played with time-honored rules by people in appropriate clothes, wearing sometimes fabulous golf shoes. It was a serious game with an illustrious past, and I loved the company of these intent men who always exuded the affable temperament and good will associated with another sublimely beautiful day on the golf course. Among the rules was a common understanding of the silence required to think about each players' next drive or putt. I learned early, right at the beginning, about the etiquette of the silence and, having perfected it, I was allowed to be there, unobtrusive and essentially invisible.

I took mental notes and paid attention, as I had been doing for years. I knew my way around the golf course and was perfectly capable of discerning any threat to its congenial atmosphere. I developed an attitude of smug ownership over this course that was essentially in my back yard, as if I was now partially responsible for its maintenance and success. I felt this responsibility so intensely that one day when I actually saw a mole cricket arrogantly appearing near one of the velvet greens, I dispatched him unceremoniously with my putter. Then I dropped his limp, pulpy body in the nearest trash can and walked away with my pointy little nose in the air to continue my patrol. These small efforts at preserving our little kingdom as a bastion of decorum endeared me even further to my father's friends. I rose in their estimation. I blossomed. It felt good, and I was happy here in a place that I understood, and that I thought understood me.

I developed a completely predictable fondness for the snack bar, the shady spot on the short seventh hole, much loved and used by nearly everyone. My father's foursome always stopped here, and I often hopped the fence separating our street from the grounds to meet him and get an ice cold Coke with a cellophane bag of peanuts poured inside the bottle. The men bought pickled eggs from a gallon jar that sat on the counter and stood around in the shade discussing their game, the merits of a short iron shot or whether the easy par 3 of number 7 had been unnecessarily complicated by a poor "lie" among the massive pine trees.

A thick forest of pines and shrubs lined the fairway, separating it from the houses of our street and from the world outside, leaving the ground covered in drifting mounds of pine straw and pine cones. It was a barrier that marked the dependable and impeccably green perfection of the course. Little affected me more than the impossibly lush and pristine fairways, elegant in those first early shadows of morning, suspended in the dewey stillness. It was just waiting, waiting for the men to come with their golf carts, clubs and lofty intentions to spend the day playing the game they loved. These were men who understood it, who played with their whole hearts, men like my father. When he became a PGA Pro a short time later, managing his own course and pro shop and teaching golf lessons, I thought how perfectly his future had finally come to him. There would be joy for him in every blade of grass and in the perfect light of that landscape, like little answers to a prayer.

The past and the present find themselves bound sometimes, inseparable by any years or events that come after them. This ground was like that, with a big story, a big past. It was the oldest golf course in Mississippi. In the early 1940's at the Gulf Coast Invitational, the golfing greats played here, including Byron Nelson and Sam Sneed in one memorable playoff people talked about for decades. But before that, long before, the ground belonged to Jefferson Davis whose beautiful home Beauvoir sat farther down the beach. These remembered figures, all from different eras, were here once and stood on this same celebrated ground. They felt the light chill that slowly descends into a mauve dusk and breathed the same salt air. In the first decades of the 1900's guests dined on seafood from local waters in the elegant rooms of the Great Southern Hotel overlooking the beach and ate salty oysters fresh from the Gulf, half-buried in cracked ice. On the white sand, friends and visitors spread out blankets and unpacked picnic hampers filled with portable feasts finished sometimes by peach hand pies and the Barq's root beer made down the beach in Biloxi.

*"There would be joy for him in every blade of grass and in the perfect light of that landscape"*

Some mornings the sun rose tranquil and indistinct on a blue gray mist that drifted thick and impenetrable, clinging to the coast so that water and sand and sky were like one thing, indistinguishable from each other. It hung dense and ghost-like among the pines, moving sometimes sideways and then upward like smoke. On these mornings the golf course emerged in a slow dawn, a hint of fairways first and then the sand traps in faint and luminous pools. The upper reaches of the pine forest only became visible slowly at the last, as if they were reluctant to be separated from the opaque mists and whatever apparitions might linger within them.

It was not difficult at all for me to imagine strong outlines of the players and galleries, dim figures dressed in the romantic clothes of the past that might still be here. Their invisible presence, the images of tourists exchanging the cold winters of Chicago or New York for the warm sea breezes off the Gulf, were subtle reminders that maybe in some ways, they had never left. I could still imagine them walking along the wide verandas and palm-filled gardens of the Great Southern Hotel even though it was gone now, or reading in the expansive spaces of the extravagant lobby. They would still embrace the celebratory mood that marked the grand beginnings of this elegant course back in 1908, their intermittent cheers and applause still alive around the oyster shell tee boxes. These imaginary apparitions of mine decorated a resplendent past. They possessed remarkable qualities; a material warmth and a tangible amiability, very much like the living who still walked the fairways in the fading afternoon light, reluctant to leave. I had my place among them all now, moving in the same unhurried way they did, making my way up the last slope toward the club house and the Gulf beyond.

Here in this green world, I found myself in an arrangement of undefinable, deliberate forces that lived here, had always lived here. To me, they were always present, always at work. My attractive, imaginary companions from past eras were at home here too, as I was, in this expanse of green, and their familiar influences were never far away. The one primary thing about a golf course was the quiet. There was a lot of time to think. Sitting cross-legged in the grass looking out at the endless Gulf, my mind drifted in the comfortable way, the effortless way, that made it easy to sift through countless things. In the silent, clear moments that came to me from the stillness, I thought this might be what freedom looked like, this green glorious park that extended the prospect of liberty all the way to the boundaries of the Gulf. I felt free here, free in all the best ways. This was no place for the lazy or half-hearted. The freedom here was used for something else, for cultivating patience and tenacity, the kind that came with its own sort of permanence. The green world all around me had a sense of infinity in it. It did its job. The protective canopy of heaven above me did its job, too. I felt completely safe here underneath the sheltering expanse of blue. It wasn't going anywhere. In the morning when my eyes opened, it would still be here.

## Chapter 9

# THE LAST DAYS

The coast was full of images to remember: the long ribbon of white beach, the grey-green moss dripping from twisted oaks that would be there long after we had all gone on, the still mornings in the shelter of an insular green world and the hours listening to the waves that were the music of this place. Those memories were mine now along with all the others and the people I wanted to remember.

My California aunt was the second personality (after my father) to gain my attention and affection. She could be surprising at times, and one afternoon I discovered she wrote poetry. You wouldn't have thought she was capable of these sentiments, writing them down over the years in small black notebooks when she had some rare moments alone. Her poems were hidden things, the kind we usually keep for just ourselves. They were her private thoughts, carefully recorded on small pages of plain paper. One day, sitting in the kitchen over our cups of tea, she offered in her quiet off-hand way to let me read them. I think now, because I loved words, and I loved her, I grasped a little bit of what those pages really represented, but not nearly enough.

I wish so much I had those pages now so I could read them with adult eyes, appreciative and understanding eyes that rewarded her for taking me into her confidence. I did praise the words and thoughts behind them, and I might have said the most horribly generic phrase possible, that those were, "really good." But she would have forgiven me, because I think she always saw what was in my heart. She was a real star, one of those who graced the stage in the early days of my life just as the curtain was going up. There were other stars and supporting cast too, who appeared with me over the years, or I was in the supporting cast of their lives, all of us delivering our lines, trying to make each of us appear at our best. But it was the small incidents sometimes, like her books of poetry, that stood out, revealing what was really there. So, she did have that one secret, at least one I knew about, and I think now her words inspired me. The act of sharing them in that unobtrusive way of hers influenced me in ways that never left me. Even then something in me wanted to write, and maybe, because nothing ever escaped her, she knew that.

My father, in addition to being a spectacular golfer was also, I discovered, a world class tap dancer, something unknown to me until one day when I was seven years old. He asked me if I would like to learn to tap dance. This appealed to me enormously, so he took me into the kitchen and began to teach me to tap dance on our green linoleum kitchen floor. I was in heaven. By the end of the afternoon I had mastered the soft shoe and the time step, and realized that I might have found my new favorite thing. My father had a surprisingly fluid style and said he had performed the soft-shoe often with sand on the floor to make it easier to slide on. Every time we tap danced in the kitchen together he taught me a whole bunch of new steps. We danced to our favorite song, "The Sidewalks of New York," and I still catch myself humming it every now and then and see us together dancing on that green kitchen floor. All those little sessions with him made me realize how much I loved dancing. I seemed to be relatively good at it and moved on from tap to ballet. He encouraged me to learn, and dance essentially became my life all the way through high school. It gave me something to love with a devotion that never left me. It became a defining thing for me, much like what golf was for him, a passion I could pursue for all the decades of my life. I have him to thank for the hours we spent being together in the kitchen, being on the golf course, and the rest of the time, just 'being.'

My French Quarter uncle introduced me to art. He handed me some pastels and a sketch pad one day and said, "Here, try sketching that flower pot over there." I made a first hesitant attempt, and it seemed fairly obvious that I would never be a serious artist. The pastels seemed unfriendly. The simple lines of the pot made me feel oddly inept, and the concept of "perspective" seemed increasingly unreachable. The subject proved illusive, escaping into an amorphous mass that might later be loosely associated with a modern abstract. My uncle was unmoved by failure. I loved this and became unmoved by failure, too. In fact, in a hostile move on its flanks, I began an aggressive attack on the flower pot, diminishing it further with every advance. After several more bold assaults, I was in secure possession of a decent picture of a flower pot, an imperfect rendering but a brilliant first try. No battle was ever fought more valiantly. My uncle and I both smiled. The mission had been successfully accomplished, and a delicious sense of achievement descended all at once into my enthusiastic little mind. I began to envision myself in a new avenue of endeavor, possibly in a vibrant and cosmopolitan atmosphere.

*"My uncle was unmoved by failure. I loved this and became unmoved by failure, too"*

I had a fleeting picture myself in a flamboyant costume painting on a large impressive canvas with broad colorful strokes in a style reminiscent of Chagal, who had just started to interest me. In my little illusionary vignette, I envisioned a quaint street filled with wildly talented artists being admired by everyone desperate to buy our brilliant work. I could already see myself, possibly in a beret, roaming the streets of Paris. The Quarter always did have a remarkable effect on one's imagination. That was part of its charm. People came here, and for one fleeting moment, they became entirely different and exciting versions of themselves. My little fantasy didn't last long, but I could depart now, carefully carrying my piece of art. I drifted into the street toward the Cathedral moving confidently among the other artists in the Quarter. I was one of them now.

The Ladies in my life worked miracles, and these miracles went largely unseen, as is often the case, occurring in the obscure recesses of their quiet home. From long years of Sunday school I knew that miracles were the exclusive expressions of God's activities. They were the dependable and trusted reflections of the divine. If there were any other lesser examples of the miraculous, I hadn't heard about them, which is why I found myself one day so unprepared. Just the barest glimpse through the kitchen door revealed one of the ladies, an elderly figure slightly bent and poised as if in worship over a pale green vessel, a small spoon balanced delicately in her thin white hand. She examined it carefully, as a scientist might evaluate an experiment, nodding a hint of satisfaction as if she was moved by some mystical force.

At that moment she sensed my presence and paused, looking over at me in the narrow doorway. "Try this," she said, coming over and handing me the spoon. I hesitated slightly, took a tiny taste, and then the miracle happened. It was mayonnaise, homemade mayonnaise, and she had just created it right there in the kitchen. It was remarkable, one of the best things I had ever tasted, and this pleasant waif-like woman had made it all by herself out of practically nothing. I was shocked. You could actually make this? "Yes," she said. I had always thought mayonnaise was a rather boring condiment that only came in jars from the grocery store. I wondered if I could learn to make this and maybe other things, too. Suddenly, in an instant, my culinary future opened like an epiphany, and I fell headlong into a new world far beyond the ubiquitous tuna casserole. I saw my future kitchen holding the heavenly dreams of buttered biscuits and scones, hummingbird cake and lemon meringue pie, the food of perpetual contentment.

The power of a warm kitchen and homemade food became clear to me that day. It was future I would enthusiastically embrace, but I would never forget that one thing. It all began with mayonnaise.

My friends, my unmatched friends from school left their own impressions in our storied past, a consummate circle of night fires and white beaches, classes and ball games. Small Sunfish sailboats took us out into the waves, bobbing in little groups against the long blue horizon of the Gulf. Lavish hours decorating floats for the Homecoming parade filled afternoons and nights. We sat on cold bleachers at the stadium, holding hands in a crisp fall darkness cheering for our football team, and we absorbed the daily encouragement of coaches and counselors. Our cars parked along the streets of our school every morning where we stood laughing and talking about everything, and nothing. Choir practice and tennis tournaments, class play rehearsals and pep rallies were history being made. It was the history of our lives, and our universe turned on a thousand ordinary things that now don't seem ordinary at all. How could we have known the importance of all those simple moments. A lifetime of memories happened there all at once, compressed into some of the best years of our lives.

Some chapters in life close so imperceptibly with the merciful and gentle slowness that one can only appreciate later. The long, shimmering months and years gathered into the warm arms of the Gulf gently lulled me and my small circle of high school friends into a semi-permanent illusion. The atmosphere, the light of the young transcendent Mississippi days was like that. It extended an invisible world, shaping our perceptions, defining who we were or who we would be. It was a light we all walked in with such clarity that all other light of future days would be measured by it. Through its innocent lens we saw our emerging universe and our place in it. There was a finality to it. It was our coming of age, a living breathing thing that we walked in.

We had the usual misfortune of youth, a vague sense that somehow these days would last forever. In the end though, our incandescent Camelot did slowly, finally slip away. The future overtook me and the ones I had come to know and love, stealing

in unobserved and only opaque at the last. I saw those buoyant days through my own rear view mirror later, distinct but receding rapidly. They were shifting impressions that I played over and over in my mind lest they be forgotten, and it was important that those images be remembered: those days, those halcyon days of salt air and moonlight, the liquid crystal of morning on the Gulf, its gray waves lapping against the last good light.

We held our class graduation party at the Edgewater Gulf Hotel, the coast's grand landmark with its iconic tower facing the Gulf. There were goodbyes, forever goodbyes, like those at our

other events and parties containing music and buffets and the first small hints of regret. There were tears and promises, talk of college and cars, walks on the beach in the perfect moonlight, and the last conversations sitting on the sea wall looking out on our Gulf. Our lives touched, overlapping for an instant, or maybe for a lifetime. We had come all this long way together, and now the friends with their shining faces began slowly slipping away into the fading light of a past that had changed us all.

We wore white dresses to our Baccalaureate and blue caps and gowns at graduation, an appropriate color for our football team, the Gulfport Commodores. We were State Big Eight Conference champions and proud of it. Some of us went to Ole Miss or Mississippi State or to the University of Southern Mississippi in Hattiesburg. Others went away out of state, and then came home to be part of the coast once more in time for Hurricane Camille, which changed our world forever, and for Hurricane Katrina which nearly finished it off. But the coast I knew retained a defining immortality, a life of its own impervious to winds and tides, unalterable by years. That permanence was its gift to us, ours to take away. It was a stamp upon our souls.

———— ⁂ ————

I went away, too, boarding a train at the station in
Gulfport, my feet standing on those white and gray,
gold and ruby mosaic tiles for the last time.
Those were the colors of this world
I was leaving: the days,
our golden days on
that white

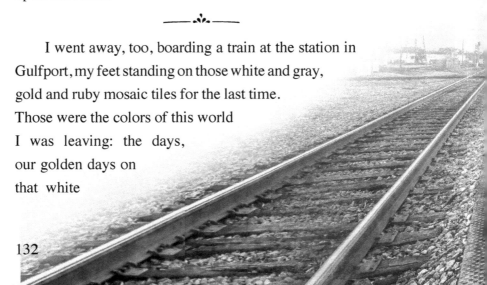

sand, and the sun, liquid red, sinking slowly into the slate gray waves of the Gulf. The trip to California, traveling on the train with my aunt, had been the fresh beginning of a liberating future. This train took me far away again into the unknown of another new future. I set out alone now, but I felt my aunt's encouraging presence, as if she might be waiting for me to join her there in the dining car for our cups of tea.

I remember carefully watching the porters loading the luggage full of all my clothes for college, and then that first exhilarating moment as the train began moving forward. I was overtaken then by those same powerful, remembered emotions of long ago, "I had been invited somewhere, and I was really going."

GRADUATION NIGHT

Those heady tides of emotion found themselves strange companions to a growing sense of regret I was unprepared for. The world I had known so happily, the world that had captured my whole heart was perched precariously on the razor thin edge of the future. It was about to become a thing I could not have imagined. It was about to become a memory.

My steps had taken me down the long blocks to the Gulf. Now for the first time, I wondered if I would see these streets again or walk into that drug store again or laugh with the saleslady when I bought a pink and green madras skirt. Would I sit here on the dock by the Yacht Club looking out at the far horizon, my thoughts of the future cradled in the rolling gray waves and lost in the ease of warm and friendly winds? I hoped I would be back. I knew the Gulf would still be here waiting for me to find myself in it. It had that reliable permanence. Yes, it had that. I felt it when I watched the streets and buildings and faces grow smaller as we pulled away from the station, slowly gathering speed, my eyes straining for the last glimpse of this place I knew.

Holding onto this moment became a little too hard, and I finally gave up, letting my mental image of the Gulf take over, being to me the familiar, comforting thing it always had been, that thing that would never leave me. Rolling on slowly, swaying in the rhythm of all trains, I watched the outskirts of our town, the town that had been mine, begin to fade, the houses giving way to pines stretching back from the long expanses between the the small Gulf communities. Even the familiar blocks of Long Beach were becoming strangers to me now as if they knew I was abandoning them. But the Gulf stayed with me all the way through Bay St. Louis. It had been here to say hello, and it was here now to say goodbye, holding me to the last in its blue embrace.

I had a pale aqua train case, a graduation gift, sitting on the seat beside me. It was new, packed with new things. I was new, too. I was a new me, with a new identity crafted from the sand, waves, salt air and benevolent sky of this place. I was now simply and forever "a girl from the coast," a novel thing at the University of Arkansas where I arrived in September of 1965, carrying Mississippi with me.

# EPILOGUE

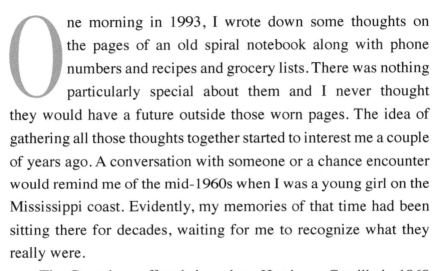

O ne morning in 1993, I wrote down some thoughts on the pages of an old spiral notebook along with phone numbers and recipes and grocery lists. There was nothing particularly special about them and I never thought they would have a future outside those worn pages. The idea of gathering all those thoughts together started to interest me a couple of years ago. A conversation with someone or a chance encounter would remind me of the mid-1960s when I was a young girl on the Mississippi coast. Evidently, my memories of that time had been sitting there for decades, waiting for me to recognize what they really were.

The Coast has suffered since then. Hurricane Camille in 1969 and Hurricane Katrina in 2005 washed away almost that entire stretch of the Gulf Coast. The house of "The Ladies," the Father Ryan House and nearly all of the grand old homes facing the beach did not survive. Even the elegant Edgewater Gulf Hotel and the Broadwater Beach Resort fell to the residual effects of the storms and changing times as did the historic Great Southern Golf Club. Only the white beach remains of the original stretch of sand where we spent our first summer. The Alamo Plaza, the Confederate Inn, the Colonial Cottages, the Friendship House, Six Gun Junction and the long fishing pier have dissolved into the mist of a cloudless past. Those memorable places have joined the storied others that anchored the long years of liquid history on a blue Gulf.

I remember the impressions of my first days here, pale sand against an unfading sunset thick with pink and gold, casting the colors of pale shrimp across the deep purple of a coming night, images I stored away, hoping I would never forget. Now decades later, the white beach shining against a pink sky over the Gulf still has the same power. It is a conspicuously unalterable atmosphere where nothing seems deteriorated or changed. The same timeless quality, with its endless capacity to comfort, reaches out invisibly to claim new souls who have come here. It welcomes them to the Mississippi Coast as it welcomed me so long ago and nurtures the ones who have always lived here in the warmth of this place.

My story has been a winding road into a past of resurrected people and places. Some memories of those golden days came back to me so clearly, while others live in a semi-gray world just beyond my reach. Hovering in the half light, the faint, well cared for images never became stale, anemic ghosts of a past. They were too real for that. I have done my best to recreate them. The main thing I hoped for when I started writing was that these people and places I loved would be honored and remembered well, with the unrestrained affection I have for them.

THE AUTHOR AND HER DAUGHTER

# RECIPES

## MAYONNAISE

INGREDIENTS

2 egg yolks
½ teaspoon red wine vinegar
2 teaspoons lemon juice
1 teaspoon Dijon mustard or dry mustard
1 cup vegetable oil or avocado oil
A pinch of salt
A pinch of pepper

Put all of the ingredients except for the oil, in a food processor fitted with a steel blade, and process them for a couple of seconds. While the machine is running, **very slowly** add the oil in a thin stream until the mixture thickens and turns into actual mayonnaise. Adjust the seasonings and put in a covered container in the refrigerator. It will usually keep for several days.

"The Ladies" in my story made this the old fashioned way, entirely by hand. I used to do this but it is a lot of work, and the results cannot be guaranteed. The results cannot be guaranteed in a food processor either. I say this as a warning to all "would be" mayonnaise makers. If the oil is not added slowly enough the mixture can "break." This event will create an eggy, oily mess that is a pain to dispose of, ruining a pleasant afternoon in the kitchen and possibly also making you dislike the person who suggested you attempt this.

When I say "add the oil slowly," I mean so slowly that decades of your life seem to pass by, and you have time to remember every detail of the most romantic date you ever had. I'm talking about eons here. Do not even contemplate bending this rule. Other than that one thing, making mayonnaise is pretty easy. Just remember that one thing.

# REALLY GOOD GUMBO

There is a lot to say about gumbo. Whole books have been written about it, and the opinions about how to make it are hotly contested. I settled on this recipe because it is just the one we all like to eat. I made gumbo for the first time in Mobile, Alabama when I had two toddlers crawling around the kitchen, and one dish meals seemed like a very practical idea. I got fresh Gulf shrimp right off the shrimp boats at the dock or sometimes down in Bayou la Batre.

## INGREDIENTS

Roux...

    1/3 cup plain flour

    1/3 cup bacon grease

Main...

    1 lb. okra

    6 cups of chicken stock

    1 green bell pepper

    1½ lb. wild caught Gulf shrimp, peeled

    1 large onion

    3 regular cans of stewed tomatoes

    4 celery stalks

    1 lb. andouille sausage, chopped

    1 lb. crab meat

    several big crab legs

Seasonings...

    1 tablespoon minced garlic   1 teaspoon creole seasoning

    1 bay leaf

    1 teaspoon thyme

    1 teaspoon oregano

    1 tablespoon dried parsley

    3 drops Tabasco sauce

The main thing about making gumbo is the roux. I know that you can buy it in jars, but making roux is a little like making mayonnaise. It's just something that I like to do. My recipe is not complicated and uses pretty basic ingredients.

Just slowly brown the flour and the bacon grease in a big heavy pot until it is a shade of brown you can live with, about the color of tobacco, but not burnt. That's all there is to it.

Once you've made the roux, set it aside and chop the okra, green bell pepper, onion, and celery. Over medium heat, stir these into the roux until ingredients are well coated.

Add the canned tomatoes, chicken stock and andouille sausage and crab legs. Next add all of the seasonings, salt and pepper to taste, and simmer over low heat for 1½ hours.

Next add the shrimp and crab meat and simmer another 20 minutes. Stir in 2 teaspoons of gumbo file' and simmer 5 minutes. Adjust seasonings and serve over cooked jasmine rice.

This recipe can be amended and added to in all kinds of ways. Enjoy!

# SWEET TEA

I know sweet tea is everywhere in grocery stores now, but my family always asks for this. I use simple syrup instead of granulated sugar which just never really dissolves, and fresh mint that I grow outside in a pot. It makes enough for a crowd, and I store it in big jars in the refrigerator.

INGREDIENTS

Simple Syrup...
- ½ cup white sugar
- 1 cup water

Main...
- 2 quarts, approximately, of brewed black tea
- 2 cans pineapple nectar
- 2 cans peach nectar
- 1 small bottle of fresh orange juice
- The juice of two lemons
- 1 large bunch of fresh mint

Simply combine the sugar and water in a medium saucepan and bring it to a boil, stirring now and then, until the sugar dissolves. Let it cool and combine remaining ingredients in two big pitchers, stirring with a wooden spoon to crush the mint and serve in iced glasses.

Hi-ball glasses can be used and garnished with pineapple chunks and maraschino cherries on cocktail spears if you want something more spectacular. Double the simple syrup if you like it really sweet.

# VIRGINIA'S COLESLAW

This is my late mother-in-law's recipe. As a new bride, I had it for the very first time at her house served with her spoon bread and ham and baked beans. It was just spectacular, and I never can eat this without thinking of her and all the recipes she shared with me.

INGREDIENTS

Base...

　8 ounces sour cream

　¾ cup good mayonnaise

　2 tablespoons apple cider vinegar

　2 tablespoons sugar

　1 teaspoon salt

　½ teaspoon black pepper

Main...

　14 ounce bag of shredded cabbage , more or less

Stir all base ingredients together with a wire whip. Combine with shredded cabbage. Cover and refrigerate. This slaw is perfect with fried catfish, shrimp po-boys, baked ham or just about anything else.

# SPOON BREAD

INGREDIENTS

- 1 cup cornmeal
- 1 ½ cups boiling water
- 1 cup milk
- 3 egg yolks, well beaten
- 3 egg whites, beaten stiff
- 1 teaspoon salt
- 2 teaspoons baking powder
- 1 tablespoon sugar
- 2 tablespoons vegetable oil

Add boiling water to cornmeal, mixing well. Allow to cool until it is luke warm. Add milk, egg yolks, salt, baking powder, sugar and vegetable oil. Mix well. Fold in stiff egg whites, combining gently. Pour into a greased 2 quart baking dish and bake at 375 degrees for 30 - 40 minutes.

The spoon bread should be slightly firm and fluffy. It is best served at once, hot and topped with butter.

This is a great side dish with ham and baked beans. Sometimes baked beans are poured right over the hot spoon bread, but I like it best by itself topped with a whole bunch of butter.

This is incredibly pleasant to eat, similar to buttered grits, and it is even good at breakfast with ham and eggs.

# CAST IRON SKILLET BISCUITS

INGREDIENTS

> ½ cup cold shortening
> 2 ½ cups self rising flour
> 1 ½ cold buttermilk
> ½ stick butter

Blend the shortening and flour together with a pastry blender until the shortening is about the size of small peas. Let it chill in the refrigerator about ten minutes. Put ½ stick butter in a 12" cast iron skillet and warm it in a 475 degree oven until the butter melts. Remove the skillet from the oven and set aside.

Make a well in the center of the flour mixture and add buttermilk. You may not need all of it. Stir until dough is combined and sticky. Don't overwork the dough. Turn the dough out onto a well-floured board. Roll out lightly with a floured rolling pin. Fold dough in half and roll it out again, adding more flour if it sticks to the rolling pin. You can repeat this a couple of more times if you're feeling energetic and you don't have hungry people waiting for those biscuits. Roll the dough to a 5/8" thickness and cut with a 2 ½ floured round cutter. Reshape scraps into biscuits.

Flip flop each biscuit in the warm butter in the cast iron skillet, pushing them close together. Usually this makes about 14-16 biscuits. If all the biscuits don't fit, I just take out a small cast iron skillet, melt some extra butter in it and put the extra biscuits in it.

Bake 15 minutes or until light golden brown in a 475 degree oven. After removing the biscuits from the oven, I cover the skillet with a heavy tea towel to help keep the biscuits warm and serve them right out of the skillet with lots more butter, honey, jam or some sort of pan gravy.

If you want to have a little more fun, use small 2" cutters and make small, hors d'oeuvres size biscuits. These make wonderful finger food when stuffed with slivers of country ham or homemade pimento cheese and arranged on trays for parties. These biscuits are nice to look at in that cast iron skillet, and they are very, very nice to eat.

# SHRIMP REMOULADE

I'm including this because the sauce is just so ridiculously good I could eat it with a spoon. It is perfect for shrimp remoulade or on fried shrimp po-boys or on avocado salad or as a dip for crab claws.

## INGREDIENTS

1 cup good mayonnaise

1/3 cup chili sauce

2-3 tablespoons creole mustard

1 tablespoon chopped garlic

3 tablespoons fresh lemon juice

¼ cup chopped green onion

2 tablespoons capers, rinsed and chopped

2 teaspoons prepared horseradish

¼ cup chopped parsley

1 teaspoon Tobasco

¼ or less teaspoon cayenne

salt and black pepper to taste

1 ½ lbs. large Gulf shrimp boiled and deveined

Iceberg lettuce, torn in small pieces

Blend all ingredients except for shrimp and lettuce in a blender. It's best refrigerated overnight, allowing the flavors to develop.

To serve, place lettuce on a salad or luncheon plate. Top with several shrimp. Pour the desired amount of sauce over the top of the shrimp. Serves four to six. This sauce will keep 3 or 4 days in the refrigerator, but you will probably eat it before that.

149

# ACKNOWLEDGMENTS

Clyde Adams, my perceptive and brilliant book designer, how deeply I appreciate your artistic vision and unending patience. Your extraordinary talent brought these pages to life and gave them a vibrance I could never have imagined. You created a path forward for my little story, and there would certainly have been no book without you. You are just, the very best.

Thank you to Ronnie Bell, classmate, friend and columnist so well known for his column "Second Thought " that he wrote for nineteen years. I am so grateful to you for reading and commenting on my pages and for a world of other advice and encouragement. To Anita Blount, my classmate, friend and Mississippi novelist, my gratitude for all the emails and the late night discussions. Mary Virginia Illingworth, librarian extraordinaire, manuscript reader, editor, full-time tea drinking literature lover and my full-time daughter, how impossible this effort would have been without you.

I am forever indebted to Betty Shaw at the Historical Society of Gulfport for so often pointing me in the right direction. My deepest thanks to the late George White for helping me with details about the Great Southern Golf Club, and to his wife, Sue for lending me the picture of the Weejuns Band. Woo Sheely, I appreciate all of your help with the Band picture. My deep appreciation to the Benefield family for permission to use your photograph. To Ellis Hill, thank you for the grand tour of the Great Southern Golf Club that was so helpful to me in remembering the course layout.

The family of the late Ron Maxie have generously shared his wonderful photographs of the Mississippi coast. I am grateful to you all for letting me use pictures taken by Ron, my classmate and friend. My indispensable resource, Oliver "Jackson" Schrumpf, cousin, friend and attorney, has generously answered so many questions. Thank you for being there for me. I appreciate, as always, my husband Gerald and my family for their limitless support and encouragement. To my father, my aunt, my uncle, the ladies and my friends from the Mississippi Gulf Coast, thank you all for giving me something to write about.

# ABOUT THE AUTHOR

Linda Carroll Barnes has been a military wife, mother, model, artist and antique store owner. A Southern woman seriously interested in a good cup of Darjeeling tea and the music of the 1940's, she loves making shrimp and grits, hot biscuits and spending as much time at the Gulf as possible.

She has lived for years in Arkansas, Louisiana, Mississippi,

Alabama and Georgia when she wasn't in far away places like Abu Dhabi or Haiti. At home now with her husband in sunny north Texas, she writes in her sunroom with a view of crepe myrtles and live oaks.

She spent her teenage years in Southern California, the French Quarter of New Orleans and on the white beaches of the Mississippi Gulf Coast, the setting of her book, *The Last Good Light: A Southern Memoir.*

# RESOURCES

More information about the Mississippi Gulf Coast is contained in the following books:

Cuevas, John. *Growing Up in Gulfport : Boomer Memories from Stone's Ice Cream to Johnny Elmer and the Rockets.* Arcadia Publishing 2019.

Cuevas, John. *Lost Gulfport.* History Press 2018.

Oliver, Nola Nance. *The Gulf Coast of Mississippi.* Hastings House 1941.

Shaw, Betty Hancock. *Gulfport.* Arcadia Pub 2011.

Tracy, Janice Branch. *Mississippi Moonshine Politics How Bootleggers & the Law Kept a Dry State Soaked.* Arcadia Publishing 2017.

John Majure

Lightning Source UK Ltd.
Milton Keynes UK
UKHW022110281222
414549UK00018B/145